Parrot Fire Kris Northern

"Rather than zoom into the fractal you can zoom into the edge of it and continually find the same pattern repeating itself much like the shoreline of a lake viewed from a plane."– **Kris Northern**

D0553486

Investigations
IN NUMBER, DATA, AND SPACE®

Editorial offices: Glenview, Illinois • Parsippany, New Jersey • New York, New York
Sales offices: Boston, Massachusetts • Duluth, Georgia
Glenview, Illinois • Coppell, Texas • Sacramento, California • Mesa, Arizona

The Investigations curriculum was developed by TERC, Cambridge, MA.

This material is based on work supported by the National Science Foundation ("NSF") under Grant No. ESI-0095450. Any opinions, findings, and conclusions or recommendations expressed in this material are those of the author(s) and do not necessarily reflect the views of the National Science Foundation.

ISBN: 0-328-23767-1

ISBN: 978-0-328-23767-8

6 7 8 9 10-V003-15 14 13 12 11 10 09 08

CC:N3

TERC

Co-Principal Investigators
Susan Jo Russell

Karen Economopoulos

Authors
Lucy Wittenberg
Director Grades 3–5

Karen Economopoulos
Director Grades K–2

Virginia Bastable
(SummerMath for Teachers,
Mt. Holyoke College)

Katie Hickey Bloomfield

Keith Cochran

Darrell Earnest

Arusha Hollister

Nancy Horowitz

Erin Leidl

Megan Murray

Young Oh

Beth W. Perry

Susan Jo Russell

Deborah Schifter
(Education
Development Center)

Kathy Sillman

Administrative Staff
Amy Taber
Project Manager

Beth Bergeron

Lorraine Brooks

Emi Fujiwara

Contributing Authors
Denise Baumann

Jennifer DiBrienza

Hollee Freeman

Paula Hooper

Jan Mokros

Stephen Monk
(University of Washington)

Mary Beth O'Connor

Judy Storeygard

Cornelia Tierney

Elizabeth Van Cleef

Carol Wright

Technology
Jim Hammerman

Classroom Field Work
Amy Appell

Rachel E. Davis

Traci Higgins

Julia Thompson

Collaborating Teachers
This group of dedicated teachers carried out extensive field testing in their classrooms, met regularly to discuss issues of teaching and learning mathematics, provided feedback to staff, welcomed staff into their classrooms to document students' work, and contributed both suggestions and written material that has been incorporated into the curriculum.

Bethany Altchek

Linda Amaral

Kimberly Beauregard

Barbara Bernard

Nancy Buell

Rose Christiansen

Chris Colbath-Hess

Lisette Colon

Kim Cook

Frances Cooper

Kathleen Drew

Rebeka Eston Salemi

Thomas Fisher

Michael Flynn

Holly Ghazey

Susan Gillis

Danielle Harrington

Elaine Herzog

Francine Hiller

Kirsten Lee Howard

Liliana Klass

Leslie Kramer

Melissa Lee Andrichak

Kelley Lee Sadowski

Jennifer Levitan

Mary Lou LoVecchio

Kristen McEnaney

Maura McGrail

Kathe Millett

Florence Molyneaux

Amy Monkiewicz

Elizabeth Monopoli

Carol Murray

Robyn Musser

Christine Norrman

Deborah O'Brien

Timothy O'Connor

Anne Marie O'Reilly

Mark Paige

Margaret Riddle

Karen Schweitzer

Elisabeth Seyferth

Susan Smith

Debra Sorvillo

Shoshanah Starr

Janice Szymaszek

Karen Tobin

JoAnn Trauschke

Ana Vaisenstein

Yvonne Watson

Michelle Woods

Mary Wright

Note: Unless otherwise noted, all contributors listed above were staff of the Education Research Collaborative at TERC during their work on the curriculum. Other affiliations during the time of development are listed.

Advisors

Deborah Lowenberg Ball,
University of Michigan

Hyman Bass, Professor of Mathematics and Mathematics Education
University of Michigan

Mary Canner, Principal, Natick Public Schools

Thomas Carpenter, Professor of Curriculum and Instruction,
University of Wisconsin-Madison

Janis Freckmann, Elementary Mathematics Coordinator,
Milwaukee Public Schools

Lynne Godfrey, Mathematics Coach,
Cambridge Public Schools

Ginger Hanlon, Instructional Specialist in Mathematics,
New York City Public Schools

DeAnn Huinker, Director, Center for Mathematics and
Science Education Research, University of Wisconsin-Milwaukee

James Kaput, Professor of Mathematics, University of
Massachusetts-Dartmouth

Kate Kline, Associate Professor, Department of Mathematics
and Statistics, Western Michigan University

Jim Lewis, Professor of Mathematics,
University of Nebraska-Lincoln

William McCallum, Professor of Mathematics,
University of Arizona

Harriet Pollatsek, Professor of Mathematics,
Mount Holyoke College

Debra Shein-Gerson, Elementary Mathematics Specialist,
Weston Public Schools

Gary Shevell, Assistant Principal,
New York City Public Schools

Liz Sweeney, Elementary Math Department,
Boston Public Schools

Lucy West, Consultant, Metamorphosis:
Teaching Learning Communities, Inc.

This revision of the curriculum was built on the work of the many authors who contributed to the first edition (published between 1994 and 1998). We acknowledge the critical contributions of these authors in developing the content and pedagogy of *Investigations*:

Authors

Joan Akers

Michael T. Battista

Douglas H. Clements

Karen Economopoulos

Marlene Kliman

Jan Mokros

Megan Murray

Ricardo Nemirovsky

Andee Rubin

Susan Jo Russell

Cornelia Tierney

Contributing Authors

Mary Berle-Carman

Rebecca B. Corwin

Rebeka Eston

Claryce Evans

Anne Goodrow

Cliff Konold

Chris Mainhart

Sue McMillen

Jerrie Moffet

Tracy Noble

Kim O'Neil

Mark Ogonowski

Julie Sarama

Amy Shulman Weinberg

Margie Singer

Virginia Woolley

Tracey Wright

Contents

U N I T   6

Decimals on Grids and Number Lines

Overview of Program Components

The **Curriculum Units** are the teaching guides. (See far right.)

Implementing Investigations in Grade 5 offers suggestions for implementing the curriculum. It also contains a comprehensive index.

The **Resources Binder** contains all the Resource Masters and Transparencies that support instruction. (Also available on CD.) The binder also includes a student software CD.

The *LogoPaths* software is formally introduced in this unit.

The **Student Activity Book** contains the consumable student pages (Recording Sheets, Homework, Practice, and so on).

The **Student Math Handbook** contains Math Words and Ideas pages and Games directions.

The *Investigations* Curriculum

Investigations in Number, Data, and Space® is a K–5 mathematics curriculum designed to engage students in making sense of mathematical ideas. Six major goals guided the development of the *Investigations in Number, Data, and Space*® curriculum. The curriculum is designed to:

- Support students to make sense of mathematics and learn that they can be mathematical thinkers

- Focus on computational fluency with whole numbers as a major goal of the elementary grades

- Provide substantive work in important areas of mathematics—rational numbers, geometry, measurement, data, and early algebra—and connections among them

- Emphasize reasoning about mathematical ideas

- Communicate mathematics content and pedagogy to teachers

- Engage the range of learners in understanding mathematics

Underlying these goals are three guiding principles that are touchstones for the *Investigations* team as we approach both students and teachers as agents of their own learning:

1. *Students have mathematical ideas.* Students come to school with ideas about numbers, shapes, measurements, patterns, and data. If given the opportunity to learn in an environment that stresses making sense of mathematics, students build on the ideas they already have and learn about new mathematics they have never encountered. Students learn that they are capable of having mathematical ideas, applying what they know to new situations, and thinking and reasoning about unfamiliar problems.

2. *Teachers are engaged in ongoing learning* about mathematics content, pedagogy, and student learning. The curriculum provides material for professional development, to be used by teachers individually or in groups, that supports teachers' continued learning as they use the curriculum over several years. The *Investigations* curriculum materials are designed as much to be a dialogue with teachers as to be a core of content for students.

3. *Teachers collaborate with the students and curriculum materials* to create the curriculum as enacted in the classroom. The only way for a good curriculum to be used well is for teachers to be active participants in implementing it. Teachers use the curriculum to maintain a clear, focused, and coherent agenda for mathematics teaching. At the same time, they observe and listen carefully to students, try to understand how they are thinking, and make teaching decisions based on these observations.

Investigations is based on experience from research and practice, including field testing that involved documentation of thousands of hours in classrooms, observations of students, input from teachers, and analysis of student work. As a result, the curriculum addresses the learning needs of real students in a wide range of classrooms and communities. The investigations are carefully designed to invite all students into mathematics—girls and boys; members of diverse cultural, ethnic, and language groups; and students with a wide variety of strengths, needs, and interests.

Based on this extensive classroom testing, the curriculum takes seriously the time students need to develop a strong conceptual foundation and skills based on that foundation. Each curriculum unit focuses on an area of content in depth, providing time for students to develop and practice ideas across a variety of activities and contexts that build on each other. Daily guidelines for time spent on class sessions, Classroom Routines (K–3), and Ten-Minute Math (3–5) reflect the commitment to devoting adequate time to mathematics in each school day.

About This Curriculum Unit

This **Curriculum Unit** is one of nine teaching guides in Grade 5. The sixth unit in Grade 5 is *Decimals on Grids and Number Lines.*

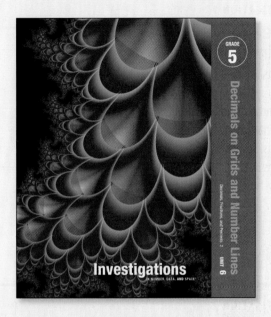

- The **Introduction and Overview** section organizes and presents the instructional materials, provides background information, and highlights important features specific to this unit.

- Each Curriculum Unit contains several **Investigations.** Each Investigation focuses on a set of related mathematical ideas.

- Investigations are divided into one-hour **Sessions,** or lessons.

- Sessions have a combination of these parts: **Activity, Discussion, Math Workshop, Assessment Activity,** and **Session Follow-Up.**

- Each session also has one or more **Ten-Minute Math** activities that are done outside of math time.

- At the back of the book is a collection of **Teacher Notes** and **Dialogue Boxes** that provide professional development related to the unit.

- Also included at the back of the book are the **Student Math Handbook** pages for this unit.

- The **Index** provides a way to look up important words or terms.

Overview

OF THIS UNIT

Investigation	Session	Day	
INVESTIGATION 1 **Understanding and Comparing Decimals** Students use their understanding of fractions and the number system to order and compare decimals to the thousandths. Grids and number lines are used as representations to learn about the relationships among decimals. Students also find decimal equivalents for fractions by dividing the numerator by the denominator.	**1.1** Decimals on Grids	1	
	1.2 Introducing Thousandths	2	
	1.3 Decimals on the Number Line	3	
	1.4 Decimals In Between	4	
	1.5 Assessment: Decimal Problems	5	
	1.6 Ordering Decimals	6	
	1.7 Fractions as Division	7	
	1.8 Decimal Equivalents	8	
	1.9 Fraction-Decimal Equivalents	9	
	1.10 Assessment: Comparing and Ordering Decimals	10	
INVESTIGATION 2 **Adding Decimals** Students use grids to help them visualize and identify the place value of decimal fractions as they begin adding decimals. Using a variety of different contexts, students add decimal fractions and consider how the addition strategies they used for addition of whole numbers apply to adding quantities less than one.	**2.1** Fill Two	11	
	2.2 The Jeweler's Gold	12	
	2.3 Strategies for Adding Decimals	13	
	2.4 Decimal Problems	14	
	2.5 Decimal Games—Part 1	15	
	2.6 Decimal Games—Part 2	16	
	2.7 Decimal Games—Part 3	17	
	2.8 End-of-Unit Assessment	18	

Each *Investigations* session has some combination of these five parts: **Activity, Discussion, Math Workshop, Assessment Activity,** and **Session Follow-Up.** These session parts are indicated in the chart below. Each session also has one or more **Ten-Minute Math** activities that are done outside of math time.

Activity	Discussion	Math Workshop	Assessment Activity	Session Follow-Up	Practicing Place Value	Estimation and Number Sense
● ● ●				●	●	
● ●	●			●	●	
● ●	●			●	●	
●	● ●			●	●	
●		●	●	●		●
		●		●		●
●	●			●		●
● ●	●			●		●
	●	●		●		●
		●	●	●	●	
● ●	●			●	●	
●	●			●	●	
●	●			●	●	
● ●	●			●	●	
●		●		●	●	
	●	●		●	●	
		●		●	●	
			●	●	●	

Ten-Minute Math

Mathematics

Decimals on Grids and Number Lines, which focuses on understanding, comparing, and adding decimals, is the sixth unit in the Grade 5 sequence and the second of two Grade 5 units in the Rational Number strand of *Investigations.* These units develop ideas about the meaning of fractions, decimals, and percents and the relationships among them; about using equivalent fractions, decimals, and percents to solve problems; about using addition and subtraction as a context to understand and use fractions and decimal fractions; and about extending understanding of place value and the base-ten number system.

LOOKING BACK In Grades 3 and 4 and in the first Rational Number unit in Grade 5, students built an understanding of the meaning of fractions and mixed numbers and developed a working knowledge of equivalent fractions and percents for fractions involving halves, thirds, fourths, fifths, sixths, eighths, tenths, and twelfths. They learned how to use equivalencies to solve problems about comparing, adding, and subtracting fractions. They used a number of representations in their work, including the area of rectangles, number lines, the area of the pattern block shapes, and rotation around a clock face. Their computation work with fractions focused on reasoning about fraction relationships and equivalencies. Students worked with tenths and hundredths in Grade 4, related them to familiar fractions (e.g., $\frac{1}{4} = 0.25$), and represented them as parts of rectangles. They found sums of decimal fractions involving tenths and some familiar hundredths such as 0.25 and 0.75.

This unit focuses on 3 Mathematical Emphases:

1 Rational Numbers Understanding the meaning of decimal fractions

Math Focus Points

◆ Identifying everyday uses of fractions and decimals

◆ Representing decimal fractions as parts of an area

◆ Reading and writing tenths, hundredths, and thousandths

◆ Identifying decimal, fraction, and percent equivalents

◆ Representing decimals by using a number line

◆ Interpreting fractions as division

◆ Interpreting the meaning of digits in a decimal number

Fractions, decimals, and percents have traditionally been taught as separate topics, each with its own rules and procedures for calculation. This unit, as well as Unit 4, emphasizes connections among these different forms of rational numbers. (See **Teacher Note:** About Teaching Decimals, Fractions, and Percents Together, page 121.) In this unit, students continue to develop their understanding of the value of decimal fractions as quantities less than one and the relationship of these numbers to fractions and percents. They extend their work with decimals to thousandths.

Students are now investigating a realm of numbers that is more difficult to visualize and contextualize; students (and, in fact, many adults) do not regularly encounter contexts in which hundredths and thousandths are used in ways that are meaningful for them. These numbers are more abstract for students than whole numbers, familiar fractions, or decimal fractions expressed in tenths. For this reason, using representations they already know and using ideas about the meaning of fractions and percents that they understand are critical. In this unit, students use the area model that they have used frequently throughout Grades

3–5 for whole numbers and for fractions and draw on the work they have done with fraction-percent equivalents.

By representing tenths, hundredths, and thousandths on rectangular grids, students learn about the relationships among these fractions—for example, that one tenth is equivalent to ten hundredths and one hundredth is equivalent to ten thousandths—and how these numbers extend the structure of tens that they understand from their work with whole numbers. (See **Teacher Note:** Extending Place Value to Thousandths and Beyond, page 123.) For example, students use their knowledge that 0.125 is equivalent to $\frac{125}{1,000}$ to shade in this quantity on a thousandths grid. Shading it on a hundredths grid shows how this number is equivalent to $12\frac{1}{2}$ hundredths. Because each column of the hundredths grid is one tenth of the area of the rectangle, this representation also shows how 0.125 is equivalent to $\frac{1}{10} + 2\frac{1}{2}$ hundredths, or $\frac{1}{10} + \frac{2}{100} + \frac{5}{1,000}$.

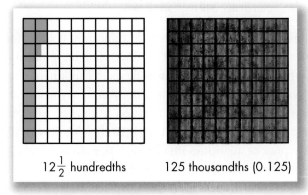

$12\frac{1}{2}$ hundredths   125 thousandths (0.125)

Sorting out these equivalencies is an important part of fifth graders' work.

Students also focus on understanding how the way we say and write these numbers is related to the meaning of the numbers. One of the difficult aspects of learning about decimal notation is that a decimal fraction is named by the smallest place. For example, 0.2 is read as "two tenths," but 0.23 is read as "twenty-three hundredths," not "two tenths and three hundredths," and 0.235 is read as "two hundred thirty-five thousandths." Students may learn to read this number correctly without the important understanding that 235 thousandths is equivalent to

2 tenths + 3 hundredths + 5 thousandths, as represented by the individual digits. Coordinating the name of the number with its meaning and equivalencies is a critical part of learning about the meaning of decimal fractions.

Understanding the meaning of zeros in decimal notation is also important. Consider these four numbers: 0.2, 0.02, 0.20, and 0.203. What does the zero represent in each case? Students sometimes say, "the zero doesn't matter;" that is, it does not affect the value of the number (e.g., they know that 0.2 = 0.2). However, thinking through the value of the zeroes in a decimal fraction is critical. When students simply "drop" the zero in 0.02 as they are adding decimals, they lose their sense of the place value of the number and end up with an incorrect sum.

One emphasis in this unit is that fractions represent division and how, by carrying out that division, students can find an equivalent decimal. Through this work, students extend their knowledge of fraction-decimal equivalents and are introduced to repeating decimals. In this context, they create a fraction-decimal table with a primary focus on halves, thirds, fourths, fifths, sixths, eighths, tenths, and twelfths, as well as some work on sevenths, ninths, and elevenths. See **Teacher Note:** Finding Decimal Equivalents of Fractions by Division, page 125 for more information.

2 Rational Numbers Comparing decimal fractions

Math Focus Points

◆ Ordering decimals and justifying their order through reasoning about decimal representations, equivalents, and relationships

◆ Comparing decimals to the landmarks 0, $\frac{1}{2}$, and 1

Students continue building on the work they did in Grade 4 and in *What's That Portion?* in Grade 5 on comparing and ordering rational numbers. Comparing and ordering decimal fractions focuses on both equivalent representations of numbers and ways to compare unequal numbers. By representing decimal fractions on rectangular grids divided into different numbers of equal parts, students learn about decimal notation that represents the same quantity. For example, by shading in 0.5 on a tenths grid, a hundredths grid, and a thousandths grid, students learn about the equivalence of 5 tenths, 50 hundredths, and 500 thousands: $0.5 = 0.50 = 0.500$.

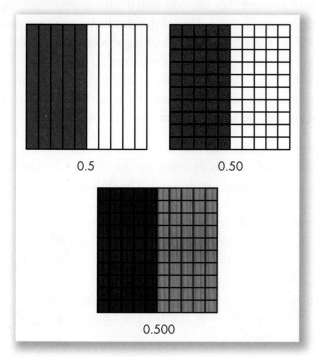

Students learn about other important relationships by representing decimal fractions on grids; for example, that 5 hundredths is equivalent to $\frac{1}{2}$ of a tenth. Students are encouraged to actually shade in the grids as they compare decimals, especially as they first work with thousandths, and then to learn to visualize this representation to help them solve problems.

Students develop and compare a variety of strategies for comparing decimals. One important way of comparing decimals is to consider the place value of the digits: 0.3 is greater than 0.248 because 3 tenths is greater than 2 tenths. Students also learn how to use decimal equivalents to compare: $0.3 = 0.300$, and 300 thousandths is more than

248 thousandths. Students use landmarks such as $\frac{1}{2}$ or 1; for example, to compare 0.489 and 0.51, students may say that 0.489 is slightly less than 0.5, or $\frac{1}{2}$, and 0.51 is slightly more than $\frac{1}{2}$. Students also use knowledge of fraction and percent equivalents to compare some decimals: because 0.05 is equivalent to 5%, it is smaller than 0.1, which is equivalent to 10%.

3 Computation with Rational Numbers Adding decimals

Math Focus Points

◆ Estimating sums of decimal numbers

◆ Using representations to add tenths, hundredths, and thousandths

◆ Adding decimals to the thousandths through reasoning about place value, equivalents, and representations

Addition of decimal fractions is an important context for learning more about decimal numbers. Solving problems that involve addition requires students to think hard about the place value of each digit in a number. They have learned many important ideas about addition from their work with whole numbers that they can apply to their work with digits that represent quantities smaller than one. In particular, students have developed whole-number addition strategies based on their understanding of the place value of the digits. As with whole numbers, students must keep track of what quantity each digit in a decimal fraction represents. For example, in order to add 0.4 and 0.124, students must know that the 4 in 0.4 and the 1 in 0.124 both represent tenths. They can represent or visualize this relationship on a rectangular grid. Students also apply their understanding of decimal equivalencies in order to add (e.g., by thinking of 4 tenths as 400 thousandths, they may add 0.400 and 0.124 as if they were adding whole numbers, but they must remember that the resulting sum represents some number of thousandths).

Students continue to use the area model to visualize addition and to support them in carefully identifying the place value of the digits in each number. When students begin to add decimals, they sometimes recognize combinations that they know from their work with whole numbers but ignore the place value of the numbers. For example, in the expression $0.07 + 0.4$, students quickly recognize the sum of 7 and 4 as 11, disregarding the place value of each of the digits—that the 4 represents tenths and the 7 represents hundredths. By representing addition of decimals on a rectangular grid, they learn to think through the place value of the numbers. They also learn about important combinations. For example, when adding 0.475 and 0.125, they notice that $0.005 + 0.005 = 0.01$ (ten thousandths is equivalent to 1 hundredth) or that $0.075 + 0.025 = 0.1$ (100 thousandths is equivalent to 1 tenth).

The goal of the work on adding decimals in Grade 5 is to strengthen students' number sense about the meaning and relationships of decimal fractions rather than to achieve computational fluency and efficient strategies. They will focus on developing fluency with decimal computation in the middle grades. Through solving addition problems in this unit, students apply their understanding of the meaning of decimals, their ideas about how to represent quantities represented by decimal fractions, and their knowledge of fraction-decimal-percent equivalencies.

This Unit also focuses on

◆ Explaining mathematical reasoning

Ten-Minute Math activities focus on

◆ Reading and writing numbers up to 100,000

◆ Adding multiples of 10 to, and subtracting multiples of 10 from, 4- and 5- digit numbers

◆ Reading and writing decimal fractions and decimal numbers

◆ Adding tenths or hundredths to, and subtracting them from, decimal fractions and decimal numbers

◆ Estimating solutions to 1- and 3-digit multiplication and division problems

◆ Breaking apart, reordering, or changing numbers mentally to determine a reasonable estimate

LOOKING FORWARD

This unit is the final unit in the curriculum that focuses on rational numbers. However, students review their work with decimal fractions on Daily Practice and Homework pages and during the Ten-Minute Math Activity *Practicing Place Value* in *Growth Patterns*. The focus of their work in the elementary grades is on understanding the meaning and equivalencies of fractions, decimals, and percents. In Grades 6–8, they build on that knowledge to develop fluency with computation involving rational numbers.

Technology Note

Using the *LogoPaths* Software If you are using the *LogoPaths* software this year, give students ongoing access to the computers **outside of math time** during this unit. *LogoPaths* Resource Masters (M1–M6) offer continued work with *Missing Measures* and *Steps* activities. Students can also continue to play *Mazes* and spend time working with the *Free Explore* option of the software. See **Part 5: Technology in *Investigations*: Calculators and Computers** in *Implementing Investigations in Grade 5:* Introducing and Managing the *LogoPaths* software in Grade 5.

Assessment

ONGOING ASSESSMENT: Observing Students at Work

The following sessions provide **Ongoing Assessment: Observing Students at Work** opportunities:

- **Session 1.1, p. 29**
- **Session 1.2, p. 36**
- **Session 1.3, p. 41**
- **Session 1.4, p. 46**
- **Session 1.5, pp. 52 and 54**

- **Session 1.7, p. 64**
- **Session 1.8, p. 70**
- **Session 1.9, pp. 75 and 76**
- **Session 2.1, p. 89**
- **Session 2.2, p. 94**

- **Session 2.3, p. 99**
- **Session 2.4, pp. 103 and 106**
- **Session 2.5, pp. 109 and 110**
- **Session 2.8, p. 118**

WRITING OPPORTUNITIES

The following sessions have **writing** opportunities for students to explain their mathematical thinking:

- **Session 1.5, p. 53**
  Student Activity Book, p. 25

- **Session 1.8, p. 72**
  Student Activity Book, p. 36

- **Session 1.10, p. 80**
  Student Activity Book, p. 42;
  M20, Assessment: Comparing
  and Ordering Decimals

PORTFOLIO OPPORTUNITIES

The following sessions have work appropriate for a **portfolio:**

- **Session 1.2, pp. 34–36**
  Student Activity Book, pp. 9–14

- **Session 1.3, pp. 38 and 40**
  Student Activity Book, pp. 16–17

- **Session 1.5, pp. 52 and 53**
  Student Activity Book, pp. 23–25

- **Session 1.10, p. 80**
  M20, Assessment: Comparing and
  Ordering Decimals

- **Session 2.3, p. 99**
  Student Activity Book, pp. 49–50

- **Session 2.8, p. 118**
  M27–M28, End-of-Unit Assessment

Assessing the Benchmarks

Observing students as they engage in conversation about their ideas is a primary means to assess their mathematical understanding. Consider all of your students' work, not just the written assessments. See the chart below for suggestions about key activities to observe.

 Checklist Available

Benchmarks in This Unit	Key Activities to Observe	Assessment
1. Read, write, and interpret decimal fractions to thousandths.	**Session 1.1:** Decimals on Grids **Session 1.2:** Representing Hundredths and Thousandths	**Sessions 1.5–1.6:** *Student Activity Book,* pp. 23–24, Problems 1–4 **Session 1.10 Assessment Activity:** Comparing and Ordering Decimals
2. Order decimals to thousandths.	**Sessions 1.4–1.6:** *Decimal In Between Game* **Sessions 1.5–1.6, 1.9–1.10:** *Smaller to Larger*	**Sessions 1.5–1.6:** *Student Activity Book,* p. 25, Problems 5 and 6 **Session 1.10 Assessment Activity:** Comparing and Ordering Decimals **Session 2.8 End-of-Unit Assessment:** Problem 1
3. Add decimal fractions through reasoning about place value, equivalents, and representations.	**Session 2.1:** *Fill Two* **Session 2.3:** Strategies for Adding Decimals **Session 2.4:** Decimal Problems **Sessions 2.5–2.7:** *Close to 1*	**Session 2.8 End-of-Unit Assessment:** Problem 2

Relating the Mathematical Emphases to the Benchmarks

Mathematical Emphases	Benchmarks
Rational Numbers Understanding the meaning of decimal fractions	1
Rational Numbers Comparing decimal fractions	2
Computation with Rational Numbers Adding decimals	3

Ten-Minute Math

Ten-Minute Math offers practice and review of key concepts for this grade level. These daily activities, to be done in ten minutes outside of math class, are introduced in a unit and repeated throughout the grade. Specific directions for the day's activity are provided in each session. For the full description and variations of each classroom activity, see *Implementing Investigations in Grade 5*.

Activity	Introduced	Full Description of Activity and Its Variations
Practicing Place Value	Unit 3, Session 1.3	*Implementing Investigations in Grade 5*
Estimation and Number Sense	Unit 2, Session 1.4	*Implementing Investigations in Grade 5*

Practicing Place Value

Students practice reading, writing, and saying numbers up to 100,000, including decimal fractions and decimal numbers to the thousandths. They add and subtract multiples of one-tenth and multiples of 10, and examine how these operations increase or decrease the values of the digits in each place.

Math Focus Points

◆ Reading and writing numbers up to 100,000

◆ Adding multiples of 10 to, and subtracting multiples of 10 from, 4- and 5-digit numbers

◆ Reading and writing decimal fractions and decimal numbers

◆ Adding tenths or hundredths to, and subtracting them from, decimal fractions and decimal numbers

Estimation and Number Sense

Students make the closest estimate they can for a problem that is created using Digit Cards and a given multiplication or division template. They explain and discuss their strategies for making good estimates.

Math Focus Points

◆ Estimating solutions to 1- and 3-digit multiplication and division problems

◆ Breaking apart, reordering, or changing numbers mentally to determine a reasonable estimate

Practice and Review

Practice and review play a critical role in the *Investigations* program. The following components and features are available to provide regular reinforcement of key mathematical concepts and procedures.

Books	Features	In This Unit . . .
Curriculum Unit	**Ten-Minute Math** offers practice and review of key concepts for this grade level. These daily activities, to be done in ten minutes outside of math class, are introduced in a unit and repeated throughout the grade. Specific directions for the day's activity are provided in each session. For the full description and variations of each classroom activity, see *Implementing Investigations in Grade 5*.	• **All sessions**
Student Activity Book	**Daily Practice** pages in the *Student Activity Book* provide one of three types of written practice: **reinforcement** of the content of the unit, **ongoing review,** or **enrichment** opportunities. Some Daily Practice pages will also have Ongoing Review items with multiple-choice problems similar to those on standardized tests.	• **All sessions**
	Homework pages in the *Student Activity Book* are an extension of the work done in class. At times they help students prepare for upcoming activities.	• **Session 1.1** • **Session 1.9** • **Session 1.3** • **Session 1.10** • **Session 1.4** • **Session 2.1** • **Session 1.5** • **Session 2.2** • **Session 1.6** • **Session 2.4** • **Session 1.7** • **Session 2.6**
Student Math Handbook	**Math Words and Ideas** in the *Student Math Handbook* are pages that summarize key words and ideas. Most Words and Ideas pages have at least one exercise.	• **Student Math Handbook, pages 54–65**
	Games pages are found in a section of the *Student Math Handbook*.	• **Student Math Handbook, pages G1, G4, G5, G7, G14**

Supporting the Range of Learners

Sessions	1.1	1.2	1.3	1.4	1.5	1.7	1.8	1.9	2.1	2.2	2.3	2.4	2.5	2.8
Intervention			•	•	•	•	•	•	•		•	•	•	•
Extension			•	•	•		•	•	•	•	•	•		
ELL	•	•								•	•	•		

Intervention

Suggestions are made to support and engage students who are having difficulty with a particular idea, activity, or problem.

Extension

Suggestions are made to support and engage students who finish early or may be ready for additional challenge.

English Language Learners (ELL)

Students continue their study of decimal fractions. Grids and place-value charts will help English Language Learners keep track of terminology such as *tenths, hundredths,* and *thousandths.* English Language Learners should be encouraged to refer to these tools when working alone or in small groups, or when participating in whole-class discussions.

In a number of activities, students are asked to express decimal fractions both as decimals (0.1) and as fractions ($\frac{1}{10}$). You may wish to meet periodically with English Language Learners to give them extra opportunities to practice these formulations. A simple exercise would be to read decimal values aloud, ask students to write each value as a decimal and a fraction, and then have students repeat each value back to you.

Throughout this unit, students are asked to explain and justify their strategies for adding decimal values. Ask English Language Learners to write down their processes and then explain to you what they did first, second, next, etc. By repeating or rephrasing their explanations, you can help English Language Learners break their strategies down into steps and articulate their ideas more clearly. So, first you added the tenths, and then you added the hundredths. Is that correct?

Give English Language Learners opportunities to preview activities and to practice expressing their ideas one-on-one or in a small group. Such practice will help English Language Learners master new vocabulary and language structures, and will allow them to participate more fully in activities and discussions with their native English-speaking peers.

Working with the Range of Learners: Classroom Cases is a set of episodes written by teachers that focuses on meeting the needs of the range of learners in the classroom. In the first section, *Setting up the Mathematical Community,* teachers write about how they create a supportive and productive learning environment in their classrooms. In the next section, *Accommodations for Learning,* teachers focus on specific modifications they make to meet the needs of some of their learners. In the last section, *Language and Representation,* teachers share how they help students use representations and develop language to investigate and express mathematical ideas. The questions at the end of each case provide a starting point for your own reflection or for discussion with colleagues. See *Implementing Investigations in Grade 5* for this set of episodes.

Mathematical Emphases

Rational Numbers Understanding the meaning of decimal fractions

Math Focus Points

◆ Identifying everyday uses of fractions and decimals

◆ Representing decimal fractions as parts of an area

◆ Reading and writing tenths, hundredths, and thousandths

◆ Identifying decimal, fraction, and percent equivalents

◆ Representing decimals by using a number line

◆ Interpreting fractions as division

◆ Interpreting the meaning of digits in a decimal number

Rational Numbers Comparing decimal fractions

Math Focus Points

◆ Ordering decimals and justifying their order through reasoning about decimal representations, equivalents, and relationships

◆ Comparing decimals to the landmarks $0, \frac{1}{2},$ and 1

This Investigation also focuses on

◆ Explaining mathematical reasoning

Understanding and Comparing Decimals

	Student Activity Book	Student Math Handbook	Professional Development: Read Ahead of Time
SESSION 1.1 p.24			
Decimals on Grids Students review the meaning of decimal notation for tenths and hundredths, and fraction and percent equivalents for decimals. They represent decimals on 10 x 10 grids.	1–6	54, 55, 58	• **Mathematics in This Unit,** p. 10 • **Part 4: Ten-Minute Math** in *Implementing Investigations in Grade 5:* Practicing Place Value • **Part 4: Ten-Minute Math** in *Implementing Investigations in Grade 5:* Estimation and Number Sense • **Teacher Note:** About Teaching Decimals, Fractions, and Percents Together, p. 121
SESSION 1.2 p. 31			
Introducing Thousandths Students develop meaning for decimal notation for thousandths, using what they know about fraction equivalents. They represent decimals on grids divided into hundredths and thousandths.	2–4, 7–15	56–57, 58, 59–60	• **Teacher Note:** Extending Place Value to Thousandths and Beyond, p. 123
SESSION 1.3 p. 37			
Decimals on the Number Line Students represent and order decimals by using a number line.	16–19	59–60, 61–62	• **Dialogue Box:** Putting Decimals in Order, p. 138
SESSION 1.4 p. 43			
Decimals In Between Students use what they know about the meaning of decimals and fraction-percent-decimal equivalents to order decimals and to play the game *Decimals In Between*.	21–22	61–62; G5	
SESSION 1.5 p. 49			
Assessment: Decimal Problems Students continue their work on ordering decimals in a two-day Math Workshop. An assessment focuses on students' reading, writing, and understanding of decimals.	23–27	54, 55–56, 61–62	

Materials to Gather	Materials to Prepare
• **Chart: "Everyday Uses of Fractions, Decimals, and Percents"** (from Unit 4) • **Chart: "Equivalents"** (from Unit 4)	• **M7–M8, Family Letter** Make copies. (1 per student)
• **Chart: "Equivalents"** (used in Session 1.1)	• **Chart Paper** Create a "Place Value" chart similar to the chart on page 6 of the *Student Math Handbook,* but with the tenths, hundredths and thousandths places *not* labeled.
	• **M11, Decimal Cards, Set A** Make copies and cut out individual cards. (1 set per pair) • **M12, Hundredths Grids** Make copies for use throughout this unit. (as needed) • **M13, Decimal Cards, Set B** Make copies and cut out individual cards. (1 set per pair) • **M9–M10, Family Letter** Make copies. (1 per student)
• **M11, Decimal Cards, Set A** (from Session 1.3) • **M12, Hundredths Grids** (from Session 1.3; as needed) • **M13, Decimal Cards, Set B** (from Session 1.3) • **Blank transparency** (optional)	• **M14, Decimal Grids** Make copies for use throughout this unit. (as needed) • **M15, *Decimals in Between*** Make copies. (as needed) • **Chart paper** Draw a sample Decimal Card layout as described in the Teaching Note on page 45. (optional)
• **M11, Decimal Cards, Set A** (from Session 1.3) • **M12, Hundredths Grids** (from Session 1.3; as needed) • **M13, Decimal Cards, Set B** (from Session 1.3) • **M15, *Decimals In Between*** (from Session 1.4; as needed)	• **M16, *Smaller to Larger*** Make copies. (as needed) • **M17, Thousandths Grids** Make copies for use throughout this unit. (as needed) • **M18, Assessment Checklist: Decimal Problems** ☑ Make copies. (1 per 6 students)

☑ Checklist Available

Understanding and Comparing Decimals, *continued*

	Student Activity Book	Student Math Handbook	Professional Development: Read Ahead of Time	
SESSION 1.6 p. 56				
Ordering Decimals Students continue their work on ordering decimals in a two-day Math Workshop.	23–25, 29–30	61–62; G14, G5		
SESSION 1.7 p. 59				
Fractions as Division Students find decimal equivalents for fractions by interpreting a fraction as division. They apply this idea to comparing win/loss records.	31–33	59–60		
SESSION 1.8 p. 66				
Decimal Equivalents Students find decimal equivalents for fractions, using what they know about fractions as well as a calculator. They make a fraction-to-decimal division table and look for patterns in the table.	35–36	59–60	• **Teacher Note:** Finding Decimal Equivalents of Fractions by Division, p. 125 • **Dialogue Box:** Filling in the Fraction-to-Decimal Division Table, p. 140; Patterns on the Division Table, p. 141	
SESSION 1.9 p. 73				
Fraction-Decimal Equivalents Students find fraction-decimal equivalents and order decimals in a 2-day Math Workshop.	35, 37–39	59–60; G14		
SESSION 1.10 p. 79				
Assessment: Comparing and Ordering Decimals Students are assessed on comparing and ordering decimals. They also finish work from the Math Workshop.	35, 37, 41–42	59–60, 61–62; G14	• **Teacher Note:** Assessment: Comparing and Ordering Decimals, p. 127	

Materials to Gather	Materials to Prepare
• **M11, Decimal Cards, Set A** (from Session 1.3) • **M13, Decimal Cards, Set B** (from Session 1.3) • **M16,** *Smaller to Larger* (from Session 1.5; as needed) • **M15,** *Decimals in Between* (from Session 1.4; as needed) • **M12, Hundredths Grids** (from Session 1.3; as needed) • **M17, Thousandths Grids** (from Session 1.4; as needed) • **M18, Assessment Checklist: Decimal Problems** ☑ (from Session 1.5)	
• **Calculators** (1 per student)	• **Chart paper** Create a chart titled "Win/Loss Records" with the information shown on page 62.
• **M12, Hundredths Grids** (from Session 1.3; as needed) • **T67, Fraction-to-Decimal Division Table** 🖳 • **T65, Decimal Grids** 🖳 • **Calculators** (1 per student)	
• **M12, Hundredths Grids** (from Session 1.3; as needed) • **M11, Decimal Cards, Set A** (from Session 1.3) • **M13, Decimal Cards, Set B** (from Session 1.3) • **M16,** *Smaller to Larger* (from Session 1.5; as needed) • **Calculators** (1 per student)	• **Chart paper** Write on chart paper the information shown on page 77.
• **M12, Hundredths Grids** (from Session 1.3; as needed) • **M11, Decimal Cards, Set A** (from Session 1.3) • **M13, Decimal Cards, Set B** (from Session 1.3) • **M16,** *Smaller to Larger* (from Session 1.5; as needed) • **Calculators** (1 per student)	• **M20, Assessment: Comparing and Ordering Decimals** Make copies. (1 per student)

🖳 Overhead Transparency   ☑ Checklist Available

Decimals on Grids

Math Focus Points

◆ Identifying everyday uses of fractions and decimals

◆ Representing decimal fractions as parts of an area

◆ Reading and writing tenths, hundredths, and thousandths

Vocabulary

fraction
decimal
percent
equivalent

Today's Plan

	Materials
ACTIVITY ① Introducing Decimals — 15 MIN, CLASS	• Chart: "Everyday Uses of Fractions, Decimals, and Percents" (from Unit 4); Chart: "Equivalents" (from Unit 4)
ACTIVITY ② Introducing Decimals on Grids — 15 MIN, CLASS, PAIRS	• *Student Activity Book,* p. 1 • Chart: "Equivalents" (from Unit 4)
ACTIVITY ③ Decimals on Grids — 30 MIN, INDIVIDUALS	• *Student Activity Book,* pp. 2–4
SESSION FOLLOW-UP ④ Daily Practice and Homework	• *Student Activity Book,* pp. 5–6 • *Student Math Handbook,* pp. 54, 55, 58 • M7–M8, Family Letter*

*See *Materials to Prepare,* p. 21.

Ten-Minute Math

Practicing Place Value Write 6,897.38 on the board and have students practice saying it. Let students know that this number is read as both "six thousand eight hundred ninety-seven and thirty-eight hundredths" and as "six thousand eight hundred ninety-seven point thirty-eight." Ask students:

• What is 20 more than 6,897.38? What is 400 more? What is 8,000 more?

Ask students how to write the new number and record it on the board. Then have them compare each sum with 6,897.38. Ask students:

• Which places have the same digits?

• Which do not? Why?

If time remains, pose additional similar problems with the numbers 895.1 and 14, 356.25.

ACTIVITY

15 MIN   CLASS

1 Introducing Decimals

To introduce this new unit, remind students of work they did in two previous units, *Thousands of Miles, Thousands of Seats* and *What's That Portion?*.

This year we have been studying our number system and working with numbers that are large, like 35,872, and small, like $\frac{1}{12}$. In this unit, we will be looking at another set of numbers that can be very small or very large: decimal numbers. These numbers extend our number system, like fractions do, to numbers that are in between whole numbers. Some of these will be familiar to you, like 0.5, and some will be unfamiliar.

Refer to the chart of "Everyday Uses of Fractions, Decimals, and Percents" from Unit 4.

Everyday Uses of FRACTIONS	Everyday Uses of DECIMALS	Everyday Uses of PERCENTS
$\frac{1}{2}$ apple	$9.95	100% on a test
$\frac{3}{4}$ inch	0.1 mile on odometer	8% tax
	0.346 batting average	20% off

Ask students for additional examples of everyday uses of decimals and add them to the list. If they do not have a variety of examples, add a few of your own.

- Rainfall in the last 24 hours: 0.25 inch

- Total rain for the month: 5.43 inches

- Car odometer: 47,364.3 miles

- Swimmer's time in 50-meter freestyle: 30.85 seconds

- Winning cyclist's average speed: 23.51 mph

Look at the decimals we have on our list. With a neighbor, read the number and discuss what the part of the number to the right of the decimal point means. Do you know any fraction it is equivalent to? What landmark is it close to, $\frac{1}{2}$ or a whole number?

Professional Development

❶ **Teacher Note:** About Teaching Decimals, Fractions, and Percents Together, p. 121

Teaching Note

❷ **Choosing Contexts** Many students can visualize this area model for decimals more easily when they have in mind a context that it might represent. Using a particular context also facilitates discussion of the representation. Choose a context for the squares used to represent decimals that is familiar to your students: a garden, a farm, or even a pan of brownies or cornbread. Make sure that the context makes it clear that each square represents 1 (1 garden, 1 farm, 1 pan of cornbread). Although the contexts are not entirely "realistic" (no one divides land or brownies in this way), students can accept these contexts as a way of visualizing the meaning of the numbers. You can even point out the humor by developing details: "Let's say that a colony of ants carries off this pan of brownies and decides to divide it up; there are many ants, so they divide the brownies into a hundred pieces. . . ."

Math Note

❸ **Writing 0 in the Ones Place** The convention we have adopted for decimal notation in the *Investigations* units is to include a zero in the ones place. Students should see numbers less than one written in decimal notation both with and without a zero in the ones place (e.g., 0.5 and .5). The zero in the ones place helps students keep track of how the decimal point separates the whole number and fractional parts. However, students should learn to recognize decimal fractions with and without the zero in the ones place.

Listen to what students understand about decimals.

- What fraction equivalents do they know (e.g., $0.25 = \frac{1}{4}$)?

- Do they know that 5.43 is almost $5\frac{1}{2}$ inches?

- Do they recognize that 30.85 is just under 31 seconds?

- Are they comfortable reading decimal notation?

Use this conversation as an opportunity to assess what your students know about decimal fractions, such as 0.25 and numbers that include a whole number and a decimal portion, such as 30.85. Expect students to vary in what they understand about decimals. Be alert to misconceptions students have and be prepared to address them as you work through the unit.❶

ACTIVITY

Introducing Decimals on Grids

15 MIN   CLASS   PAIRS

Students worked with decimal fractions in tenths and hundredths in Grade 4. In this session, students review the meaning of those numbers by interpreting representations of them on a 10 × 10 grid. Students used this representation in Grade 4 and should be familiar with it. If you find that students are very comfortable with hundredths, you can move more quickly through this introduction, but it is usual for fifth graders to need some time to review the meaning of tenths and hundredths.

Ask students to look at the top two grids on *Student Activity Book* page 1. Focus on the first square, divided into tenths, and establish that it is one whole by using the context of a large garden or farm divided into different sections.

Here's a large garden divided into different plots. Let's say that this shaded part is planted with tomatoes and the rest is planted with lettuce. What part of the garden is planted with tomatoes? How would you say this with a fraction, a percent, or a decimal?❷ ❸

As students suggest different ways to represent this amount, record them.

$$\tfrac{1}{2} = 50\% = 0.5 = \tfrac{5}{10}$$

Ask students to look at the second square, divided into hundredths.

Here's another garden that's the same size. The shaded part is also planted with tomatoes. How much of this garden is planted with tomatoes?

The purpose of this comparison is to establish that $\tfrac{50}{100}$ is another way to name this amount, that it can also be written as a decimal (0.50), and that these numbers are all equivalent. Add these numbers to what you have already written on the class "Equivalents" chart as students suggest them, or, if students do not bring them up, bring them up yourself and ask students what they mean.

$$\tfrac{1}{2} = 50\% = 0.5 = \tfrac{5}{10} = \tfrac{50}{100} = 0.50$$

How do you know that 5 tenths and 50 hundredths are equal?

Students can look at the two squares to help them describe how they know that $\tfrac{5}{10} = \tfrac{50}{100}$.

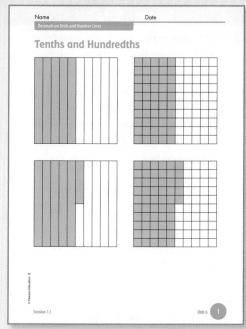

▲ **Student Activity Book, p. 1**

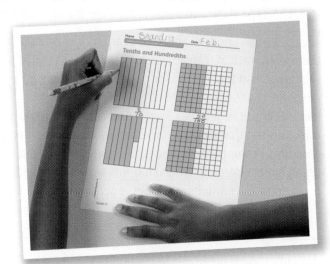

On Student Activity Book *page 1, students begin to explore relationships between equivalent fractions and decimals.*

Math Note

❹ Reading Decimals Some students may read the decimals as "point five" and "point fifty-five." Such a reading is correct, but to help students with understanding the place value of decimals and the connection between decimals and fractions, ask them to read the numbers as "five tenths" and "fifty-five hundredths." Use this language throughout the unit.

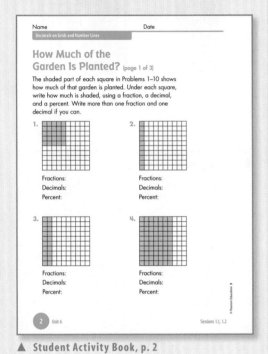

▲ Student Activity Book, p. 2

Now look together at the third and fourth squares.

Here are two more gardens. The shaded parts are planted with corn. What part of each garden is planted with corn? How many ways do you know to write a number for that part of the garden?

Students discuss this question with a partner for a few minutes. Then collect the ways students know to write the fractional part of the gardens and ask them to explain the meaning of these numbers.❹

How do you know that 55% of the garden is planted in corn? What does 0.55 mean?

Some students may recognize that 0.55 means 55 hundredths; others may also know that the first five means 5 tenths (which is equivalent to 50 hundredths) and that the second five means 5 hundredths. By looking at the square divided into tenths, students notice that this part of the garden is $5\frac{1}{2}$ tenths. If students come up with these ideas, add them to your list:

$$\frac{55}{100} = 55\% = 0.55 = 0.50 + 0.05 = \frac{5}{10} + \frac{5}{100} = \frac{5\frac{1}{2}}{10}$$

DIFFERENTIATION: Supporting the Range of Learners

ELL English Language Learners can create visual aids to help them keep track of relevant vocabulary. Explain that a garden plot is a section of land that is used for planting and growing vegetables. What are some vegetables that might grow in a *garden plot?* Show students pictures of the vegetables used in this activity: *tomatoes, lettuce,* and *corn.* Suggest that students create a key for their garden plot by choosing a color to represent each vegetable (e.g., red for *tomatoes,* green for *lettuce,* etc.). When students work with a grid, they can color in sections to show where certain vegetables grow.

ACTIVITY

30 MIN INDIVIDUALS

③ Decimals on Grids

Students work on *Student Activity Book* pages 2–4. This activity continues the review of decimal fractions in tenths and hundredths as parts of an area and equivalent ways to write them—as fractions, percents, and decimals.

As students work, observe which parts of an area students can easily recognize and notate as decimal fractions and which cause some difficulty. Problems from these pages are discussed at the beginning of Session 1.2.

On Student Activity Book *pages 2–4, students use the visual aid of the grid to develop their sense of equivalent decimals.*

✔

ONGOING ASSESSMENT: Observing Students at Work

Students identify different fractional parts of a square and ways to represent them by using fractions, percents, and decimals.

- **Are students able to identify each shaded portion?**

- **Do students recognize familiar fraction-decimal equivalents, such as $\frac{1}{4} = 0.25$ and $\frac{3}{4} = 0.75$?**

- **Are students able to correctly write the fractions for parts of the square, using tenths or hundredths ($\frac{7}{10}$, $\frac{65}{100}$)?**

- **Are students able to write the number for each portion, using decimal notation?**

- **Do students know the relationship between tenths and hundredths; for example, that one tenth equals ten hundredths?**

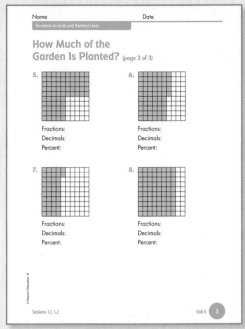

▲ **Student Activity Book, p. 3**

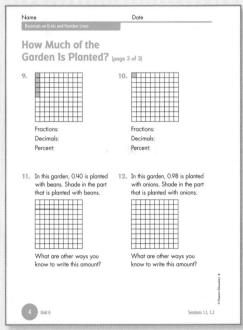

▲ **Student Activity Book, p. 4**

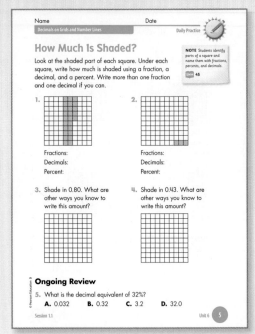

▲ Student Activity Book, p. 5

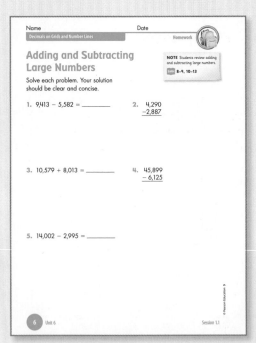

▲ Student Activity Book, p. 6

Observe students as they work, and ask them to explain their thinking. Ask questions such as these:

- How did you figure out how much of the grid is shaded? How did you determine the equivalent decimal, fraction, and percent?

SESSION FOLLOW-UP

④ Daily Practice and Homework

Practice: For reinforcement of this unit's content, have students complete *Student Activity Book* page 5.

Homework: Students solve 4- and 5-digit addition and subtraction problems on *Student Activity Book* page 6.

Student Math Handbook: Students and families may use *Student Math Handbook* pages 54, 55, 58 for reference and review. See pages 147–151 in the back of this unit.

Family Letter: Send home copies of Family Letter (M7–M8).

Introducing Thousandths

Math Focus Points

◆ Representing decimal fractions as parts of an area

◆ Reading and writing tenths, hundredths, and thousandths

◆ Identifying decimal, fraction, and percent equivalents

Vocabulary

tenths
hundredths
thousandths

Today's Plan		Materials
DISCUSSION ❶ **Place Value of Tenths and Hundredths**	15 MIN CLASS	• *Student Activity Book,* pp. 2–4 (from Session 1.1)
ACTIVITY ❷ **Introducing Thousandths**	15 MIN CLASS PAIRS	• Chart: "Place Value"* • Chart: "Equivalents" (from Session 1.1) • *Student Activity Book,* pp. 7–8
ACTIVITY ❸ **Representing Hundredths and Thousandths**	30 MIN INDIVIDUALS	• *Student Activity Book,* pp. 9–14
SESSION FOLLOW-UP ❹ **Daily Practice**		• *Student Activity Book,* p. 15 • *Student Math Handbook,* pp. 56–57, 58, 59–60

*See *Materials to Prepare,* p. 21.

Ten-Minute Math

Practicing Place Value Write 990.05 on the board and have students practice saying it. Let students know that this number is read as both "nine hundred ninety and five hundredths" and as "nine hundred ninety point zero five." Ask students:

• What is 50 less than 990.05? What is 10 more? What is 200 more?

Ask students how to write the new number and record it on the board. Then have them compare each sum or difference with 990.05. Ask students:

• Which places have the same digits?

• Which do not? Why?

If time remains, pose additional similar problems with the numbers 80.45 and 6,590.03.

Math Note

❶ **Zeros in Decimal Notation** Many students need a great deal of experience sorting out the meaning of zeros in decimal fractions, just as younger students need time to sort out the meaning of zeros in whole numbers. Students encounter zero in the ones place (e.g., 0.3), zero in the place farthest to the right (e.g., 0.250), and zero between or to the left of other digits in a decimal fraction (e.g., 0.05 or 0.506). You may hear students say "the zero does not matter" when referring to 0.3 or 0.250, by which they mean that the value of the number is not changed if the zero is ignored or removed (0.3 = .3 and 0.250 = 0.25). However, some students apply this "zero doesn't matter" idea to *any* zero, which leads to incorrect interpretations of the values of the numbers and to incorrect computation with decimals. Help students develop the habit of articulating what all of the digits in a decimal fraction mean, including any zeroes, no matter where they occur in the number.

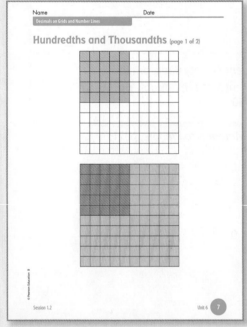

▲ Student Activity Book, p. 7

DISCUSSION
1 Place Value of Tenths and Hundredths

⏱ 15 MIN 👥 CLASS

Math Focus Points for Discussion

◆ Representing decimal fractions as parts of an area

Choose one or two of the problems from *Student Activity Book* pages 2–4 to discuss. You can choose according to which of the problems students found most difficult. Ask questions such as:

• How much of the garden is planted? How do you know? How would you write that as a fraction? As a percent? As a decimal?

• What does the 6 in 0.65 mean? What does the 5 mean?

• If you were going to say how many tenths of this garden is planted, how would you say that?

• How do you know that 5 hundredths is equal to $\frac{1}{2}$ of a tenth?

Focus on Problems 2 and 10, and ask students the different ways they wrote the parts of the garden for these problems. Ask questions to draw attention to the two places—tenths and hundredths.

• What does 0.1 mean? What does 0.01 mean? How are they different?

• What would 0.11 mean? ($\frac{11}{100}$ or $\frac{1}{10} + \frac{1}{100}$) How can 0.11 mean both $\frac{11}{100}$ and $\frac{1}{10}$ plus $\frac{1}{100}$?

DIFFERENTIATION: Supporting the Range of Learners

ELL English Language Learners will benefit from additional opportunities to practice identifying and naming place values for decimal fractions. One-on-one or in a small group, review place names for decimal fractions up to *hundredths*. Then ask students to write simple values both as factions and as decimals. How do we write the value "three tenths" as a fraction? ($\frac{3}{10}$) How could we write the same value as a decimal? (0.3) Have students refer to a Place Value chart as a visual aid. (Students will learn about thousandths in the next activity. You can preview this term by including it in these practice exercises.)

ACTIVITY

② Introducing Thousandths

15 MIN · CLASS · PAIRS

Write a number in the 10,000s on the board, such as the following:

79,321

Take a minute to review the names of the places and their values for this number (e.g., the 7 represents 7 ten thousands, the 9 represents 9 thousands, and so on). Then add a decimal point and two numbers representing tenths and hundredths, as follows:❶

79,321.45

Ask what the numbers in the tenths and hundredths places represent.

What does the 4 mean? What does the 5 mean? How would you read this number? If you were putting this number on a number line, where would it go? After what number? Before what number?

Then draw students' attention to the "Place Value" chart you prepared ahead of time.

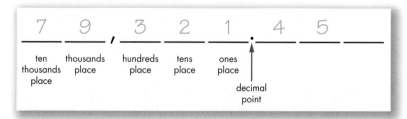

Ask students what you should label the tenths and hundredths places. Then ask them to look at what they have so far and point to the (unlabeled) thousandths place.❷ ❸

What do you think this place should be labeled? If I put a number here, what would it mean? What do you notice about the names of the places? What does the 2 in the tens place mean? What number does it represent? How is that different from the 4 in the tenths place? What number does that represent? If I put a number here in the thousandths place, what do you think it would represent?

Students may notice that there is a certain symmetry in the names of places to the left and right of the ones place: a number in the *tens* place represents that number of tens (e.g., 2×10), whereas a number in the *tenths* place represents that number of tenths (e.g., $4 \times \frac{1}{10}$).

If students are not sure what a number in the thousandths place would mean, leave it unlabeled until students look at the thousandths grids.

Professional Development

❷ **Teacher Note:** Extending Place Value to Thousandths and Beyond, p. 123

Math Note

❸ **Place Values Less Than One** Although fractions can have any denominator—thirds, twelfths, thirty-sevenths—decimals are an extension of the place-value system and one fraction equivalent for any rational number in decimal form will always have a denominator that is a power of ten. Throughout the unit, emphasize how decimals are an extension of the place-value system and based on a system of tens. A key idea is that decimals are often easier to use for computation because they are always expressed in powers of 10—tenths, hundredths, thousandths, and so on.

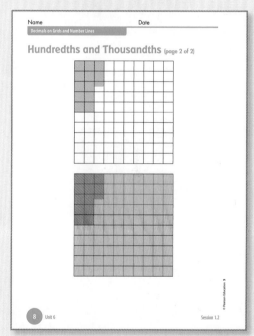

▲ **Student Activity Book, p. 8**

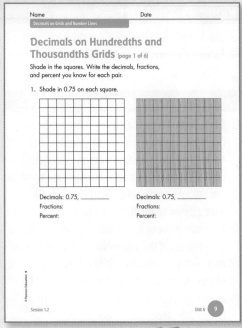

▲ **Student Activity Book, p. 9** PORTFOLIO

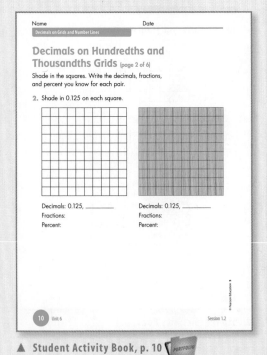

▲ **Student Activity Book, p. 10** PORTFOLIO

Now look with students at *Student Activity Book* page 7. As you did in Session 1.1, use the context you have chosen (a garden is used as the example here) and ask about the shading of the two gardens.

Look at the two gardens on this page. Let's say that the shaded part of each garden is planted with peas. What part of each garden is planted with peas? How would you write this amount with a fraction, a percent, or a decimal? Make sure that you figure out how many parts the second square is divided into and how many of those parts are shaded.

Students work with a partner for a few minutes to determine what part of the garden is shaded and to record equivalent ways to write this amount. As students work, make sure that they figure out the total number of parts in the second square *(1,000)*.

Ask for students' ideas and write the equivalents they have come up with. Focus the discussion on the number of hundredths and thousandths and the way to write them as decimals.

How many parts does the second garden have altogether? How many of those parts are planted? How would you write that as a fraction? How do you think you would write that as a decimal?

As students suggest different ways to represent this amount, record them on the "Equivalents" chart.

$$\frac{1}{4} = 25\% = \frac{25}{100} = 0.25 = \frac{250}{1,000} = 0.250$$

Focus the discussion on why 25 out of 100 equal parts of the square is equivalent to 250 out of 1,000 parts of the square and how 0.25 and 0.250 both represent this amount.

Some students may recognize that the part shaded is also $2\frac{1}{2}$ tenths. If students come up with this idea, add it to your list.

Now ask students to look at the two squares on *Student Activity Book* page 8 to discuss with a partner how much of each garden is shaded, and to record the amount as fractions, decimals, and percents. Again, make sure that they think about how many parts out of a thousand are shaded.

Collect the ways students have come up with for the shaded amount (they should know the fraction and percent equivalents from their work in Unit 4).

$$\frac{1}{8} = 12\frac{1}{2}\% = \frac{125}{1,000} = 0.125$$

Focus the discussion on the meaning of the decimal 0.125.

Students might say:

 "It's 125 out of 1,000 parts, so I can write it as $\frac{125}{1,000}$."

 "$12\frac{1}{2}$% means 12 and $\frac{1}{2}$ hundredths, so the decimal kind of means the same thing."

 "0.125 means one tenth and two hundredths and 5 thousandths."

Refer back to the "Place Value" chart, and label the thousandths place. Summarize the introduction to thousandths.

One thousandth is one out of one thousand equal parts, like one of those tiny sections of the garden. How would you write one thousandth as a decimal?

ACTIVITY

③ Representing Hundredths and Thousandths

30 MIN INDIVIDUALS

Students work on *Student Activity Book* pages 9–14. So far, students have been identifying parts of a whole shown as shaded parts of a square. Now, students are given a decimal number and use the squares to represent that number.

As needed, remind students to think about fraction and percent equivalents that they know to help them. Remind them to think about a context if that is useful, as they think about how much of each grid to shade. Help students record the shaded parts of the grid in both hundredths and thousandths. For example, in Problem 1, 0.75 is already provided as a decimal, but it can also be expressed as $\frac{75}{100}$. For the second square, the fractional part can be expressed as $\frac{750}{1,000}$ or 0.750. (Although 0.75 is also correct for the second square, students should get used to thinking of 0.75 as both 75 hundredths and 750 thousandths for more flexibility when they compare decimals in the next few sessions.)

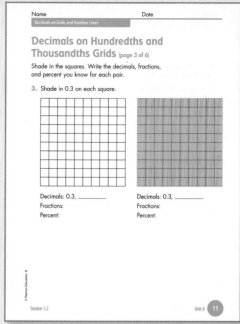

▲ **Student Activity Book, p. 11**

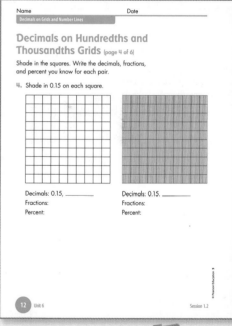

▲ **Student Activity Book, p. 12**

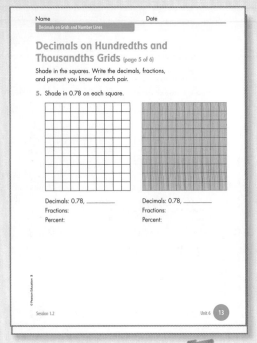

ONGOING ASSESSMENT: Observing Students at Work

Students shade in parts of a square to represent decimal fractions in the hundredths and thousandths.

- **Are students able to identify each shaded portion?** Can they correctly shade in partial squares on the hundredths grid for 0.125 and 0.625?

- **Do students recognize familiar fraction-decimal-percent equivalents, such as $\frac{3}{4} = 0.75 = 75\%$?**

- **Are students able to correctly write the fractions for parts of the square, using tenths, hundredths, and thousandths (e.g., $\frac{3}{10}, \frac{30}{100}, \frac{300}{1,000}$)?**

- **Are students able to correctly write the decimals for parts of the square, using tenths, hundredths, and thousandths (e.g., 0.3, 0.30, 0.300)?**

- **As students use the grids, are they becoming aware of the relationships between tenths, hundredths, and thousandths (e.g., that one tenth equals ten hundredths or 100 thousandths and that one hundredth equals ten thousandths)?**

Observe students as they work, and ask them to explain their thinking. Ask questions such as these:

- How did you decide how much of the grid to shade in?

- How did you determine the equivalent decimal, fraction, and percent?

▲ Student Activity Book, pp. 13–14

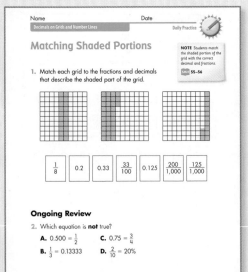

▲ Student Activity Book, p. 15

SESSION FOLLOW-UP

Daily Practice

Daily Practice: For reinforcement of this unit's content, have students complete *Student Activity Book* page 15.

Student Math Handbook: Students and families may use *Student Math Handbook* pages 56–57, 58, 59–60 for reference and review. See pages 147–151 in the back of this unit.

Decimals on the Number Line

Math Focus Points

◆ Representing decimals by using a number line

◆ Identifying decimal, fraction, and percent equivalents

◆ Ordering decimals and justifying their order through reasoning about decimal representations, equivalents, and relationships

Vocabulary

ten thousandths
number line

Today's Plan

	Materials
❶ DISCUSSION **Decimal Equivalencies** 10 MIN · CLASS · PAIRS	• *Student Activity Book,* p. 16
❷ ACTIVITY **Introducing Decimals on a Number Line** 10 MIN · CLASS · PAIRS	• *Student Activity Book,* p. 16
❸ ACTIVITY **Ordering Tenths and Hundredths** 40 MIN · PAIRS · INDIVIDUALS	• *Student Activity Book,* p. 17 • M11–M13*
❹ SESSION FOLLOW-UP **Daily Practice and Homework**	• *Student Activity Book,* pp. 18–19 • *Student Math Handbook,* pp. 59–60, 61–62 • M9–M10, Family Letter*

*See *Materials to Prepare,* p. 21.

Ten-Minute Math

Practicing Place Value Say "twelve thousand six hundred seventy-five and five tenths," and ask students to write the number. Make sure that all students can read, write, and say this number correctly. Ask students to solve these problems mentally, if possible:

• What is 12,675.5 + 800? 12,675.5 + 8,000? 12,675.5 − 2,000? 12,675.5 − 200?

Have students compare each sum or difference with 12,675.5. Ask students:

• Which places have the same digits?

• Which do not? Why?

If time remains, pose additional similar problems with the numbers 42,534.89 and 23,790.6.

Decimal Grids

Tenths

Hundredths

Thousandths

Ten Thousandths

16 Unit 6   Session 1.3

▲ Student Activity Book, p. 16;
Resource Masters, M14; T65

① Decimal Equivalencies

10 MIN   CLASS   PAIRS

Math Focus Points for Discussion

◈ Identifying decimal, fraction, and percent equivalents

Ask students about equivalencies among tenths, hundredths, and thousandths as they look at *Student Activity Book* page 16.

Let's again think of these squares as gardens divided into different plots for different vegetables, trees, or flowers. By looking at these four gardens, let's see what we can say about the relationship between tenths, hundredths, and thousandths. For example, let's say I planted one tenth of the first garden with watermelon, one tenth of the second garden with watermelon, and one tenth of the third garden with watermelon. What are all the ways you can use decimals, fractions, and percents to describe how much of each garden I planted with watermelon?

Students talk with a partner for a few minutes. If they wish, they can shade in one tenth on each grid. Then collect student ideas and write different ways to record one tenth on the board.

$$0.1 = \tfrac{1}{10} = \tfrac{10}{100} = 0.10 = 10\% = \tfrac{100}{1,000} = 0.100$$

Ask students to explain their responses by referring to the grids.

How did you figure out how many thousandths are in one tenth?

Now ask about equivalents for one hundredth. Ask students to talk in pairs and then share ideas in the same way as for one tenths.

Some students may also be interested in the ten-thousandths grid and may come up with equivalents involving ten thousandths (e.g., one tenth is equivalent to 1,000 ten thousandths). You can record these as well, but do not spend much time on this grid in this discussion.

ACTIVITY

② Introducing Decimals on a Number Line

Draw this number line on the board:

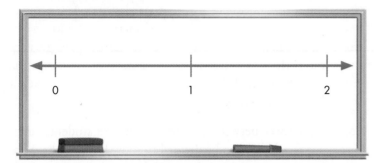

We've used number lines before, and now we're going to use a number line to represent decimals. You can see that this number line has 0, 1, and 2 marked. What if we wanted to show 0.6 on the number line? How would we do that? Talk with a neighbor.

Give students time to discuss this, and then ask a student to explain where 0.6 should be marked.

Everyone seems to agree that 0.6 will be between 0 and 1. More specifically, someone suggested that it will be slightly more than halfway between 0 and 1. What if we wanted to be more precise and place 0.6 as close as we can to where it belongs between 0 and 1? How could we make our number line more precise?

Give students time to discuss this, and then ask a student to explain how the number line could be marked. Mark the number line in tenths to demonstrate.

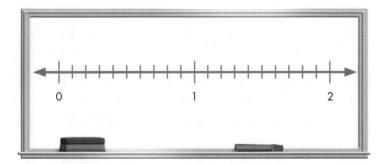

Write these decimals on the board: 0.3, 0.5, 1.25, 1.8.

Professional Development

❶ Dialogue Box: Putting Decimals in Order, p. 138

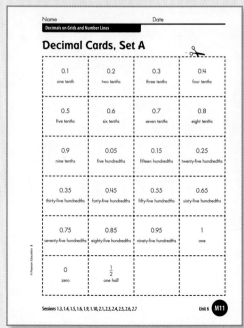

▲ **Resource Masters, M11; T62**

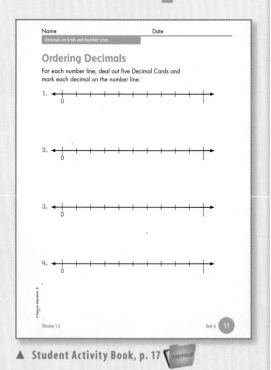

▲ **Student Activity Book, p. 17**

Ask students to draw their own number lines, including tenths, and to label these four decimals. After a few minutes, ask students to come to the board or overhead and label the decimals. Labeling 1.25 is likely to cause uncertainty for some students. Ask students to share their ideas about the value of 1.25, including equivalents they know.

I wonder if some of you found placing 1.25 to be a challenge. Let's think about this number. Is it more or less than 1.2? How do you know? . . . Is it more or less than 1.3? How do you know? . . . Does thinking about what 0.25 looks like on our 10 × 10 grids help you think about this? . . . So it sounds like most of you agree that it is going to be between 1.2 and 1.3, and some of you are even saying that it will be exactly halfway.

Point to the space between 1.2 and 1.3 and ask students how many times that space would have to be divided to show hundredths. Some students will know right away that it is ten. Other students may refer back to the grids on *Student Activity Book* page 16. If others seem unconvinced, ask them to consider how hundredths could be shown on the part of the line from 1 to 2.

Students get more experience ordering decimals on a number line in the next activity.

ACTIVITY

40 MIN   PAIRS   INDIVIDUALS

③ Ordering Tenths and Hundredths

Students use Decimal Cards, Set A (M11), for this activity. (Remove 0, $\frac{1}{2}$, and 1 from the set.) Have students look at the cards and talk briefly with a neighbor about what they notice. Students should notice that the cards show numbers that are tenths and hundredths, and they may notice that the cards start with five hundredths and go to 95 hundredths in increments of 5 hundredths (0.05, 0.1, 0.15, 0.2, and so on).

With a partner, students mix up the cards and then work together to put them in order from least to greatest. Encourage students to put the five-tenths card in the middle and use $\frac{1}{2}$ as a landmark.❶

Students use knowledge of the number system and fractions to place decimal cards in order.

After students have put all of the cards in order, they should ask you to check their ordering or check it with another pair of students. Students then complete *Student Activity Book* page 17.

ONGOING ASSESSMENT: Observing Students at Work

Students place decimals in order.

- **Are students able to place the numbers in the correct order?** If not, which comparisons are difficult for them?

- **Are students able to correctly place the numbers on the number lines marked with tenths?** Do they know that a number with 5 in the hundredths place goes between the tenths marks on the number line (e.g., 0.15 is one and one half tenths)?

- **Are students able to place the decimals in approximately the correct place on the unmarked number line (e.g., 0.95 is close to 1, 0.25 is at $\frac{1}{4}$)?**

If students are having difficulty placing the numbers with 5 in the hundredths place, such as 0.35, ask them to show you how they would represent the number on the hundredths grid on *Student Activity Book* page 16. Then they should compare that number with the tenths grid: is it more or less than 3 tenths? 4 tenths?

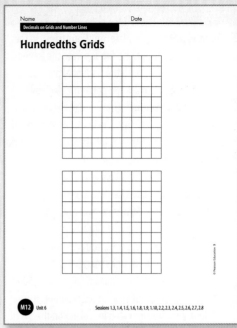

▲ Resource Masters, M12; T63

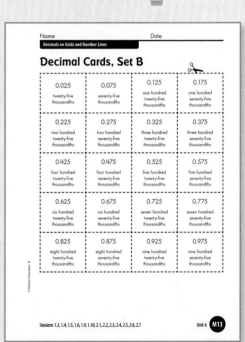

▲ Resource Masters, M13; T64

Math Note

 Decimal Notation in Different Countries In the United States, a dot is used to separate the integer part of the number from the fractional part. Some other countries also use the dot as the decimal separator; these include China, India, Ireland, Japan, Mexico, Nigeria, Pakistan, Thailand, and the United Kingdom. In many other countries (including Bolivia, Brazil, Chile, France, Germany, Italy, Peru, Poland, Russia, South Africa, and Venezuela), a comma is used as the decimal marker and a space or period is used to demarcate the whole number portions of a number; for example; 22,222.22 is written as 22 222,22 in some countries. You may want to ask students to interview family members about the way they write a number such as 10.25 and 1,500.5 and post the different ways in your classroom. Students may be interested in looking on the Internet under "decimal notation" to find more information.

DIFFERENTIATION: Supporting the Range of Learners

Intervention If some students are having a great deal of difficulty putting the numbers in order, choose about six of the cards for them to shade in on hundredths grids, using Hundredths Grids (M12). Then they decide how to put those six in order. Make sure that the cards include some hundredths and numbers in tenths they are close to. For example, you may give them the mixed-up cards 0.15, 0.2, 0.25, 0.5, 0.55, and 0.95. Then give them a few more cards to add into their ordering (which they can again shade in first on grids, if they choose).

Extension Students who easily complete the ordering task and easily place numbers on the first two number lines on *Student Activity Book* page 17 can use Decimal Cards, Set B (M13) for the third and fourth number lines. It is difficult to show thousandths on the number line, but students will still be able to estimate their position and to show the correct sequence.

SESSION FOLLOW-UP

Daily Practice and Homework

 Daily Practice: For ongoing review, have students complete *Student Activity Book* page 18.

Homework: Students practice putting decimals in order on *Student Activity Book* page 19.

Student Math Handbook: Students and families may use *Student Math Handbook* pages 59–60, 61–62 for reference and review. See pages 147–151 in the back of this unit.

Family Letter: Send home copies of Family Letter (M9–M10).

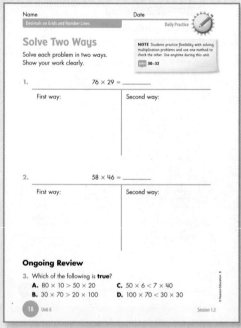

▲ Student Activity Book, p. 18

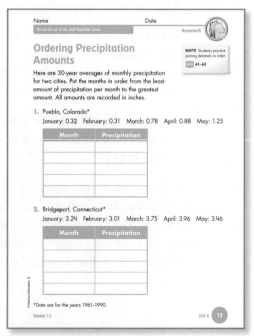

▲ Student Activity Book, p. 19

Decimals In Between

Math Focus Points

◆ Ordering decimals and justifying their order through reasoning about decimal representations, equivalents, and relationships

◆ Comparing decimals to the landmarks 0, $\frac{1}{2}$, and 1

Today's Plan		Materials
① DISCUSSION **Which is Greatest?**	15 MIN · CLASS	• M14* • Chart paper (optional)
② ACTIVITY ***Decimals In Between* Game**	30 MIN · CLASS · PAIRS	• M11–M13; M14–M15*
③ DISCUSSION **Comparing Decimals**	15 MIN · CLASS	• M11; M13; M14
④ SESSION FOLLOW-UP **Daily Practice and Homework**		• *Student Activity Book*, pp. 21–22 • *Student Math Handbook*, pp. 61–62; G5

*See *Materials to Prepare*, p. 21.

Ten-Minute Math

Practicing Place Value Say "sixty-two thousand forty-eight and seven hundredths," and ask students to write the number. Make sure that all students can read, write, and say this number correctly. Ask students to solve these problems mentally, if possible:

• What is 62,048.07 + 200? 62,048.07 − 200? 62,048.07 + 2,000?

Have students compare each sum or difference with 62,048.07. Ask students:

• Which places have the same digits?

• Which do not? Why?

If time remains, pose additional similar problems with the numbers 10,005.95 and 158,649.3.

Teaching Note

① Contexts for Comparing Decimals For many students, visualizing a context helps them think about the meaning of decimal fractions. It is difficult to find contexts that students have either experienced or can imagine in which measurements are made that involve thousandths. One that students might recognize is the measurement for the standard beverage can that holds 0.355 liter (355 milliliters). Students can picture a liter container of a beverage, and can visualize that a beverage can holds $\frac{355}{1,000}$ of that amount—a little more than $\frac{1}{3}$. Using the beverage can as a benchmark may help with thinking about other quantities (e.g., 0.125 liter is close to $\frac{1}{3}$ of the amount in a beverage can). One of the few sports that measures records to thousandths is short-track ice speed skating. As of October 2005, the men's record for a 500-meter race was 41.184 seconds and the women's record was 43.671 seconds (source: http://www.infoplease.com/ipsa/A0112785.html). Here is a question you could pose in this context that might help some students think and talk about the problem in this discussion: "Suppose four ice speed skaters had these times in a race: 45.125 seconds, 45.25 seconds, 45.02 seconds, and 45.3 seconds. Who had the fastest time? How do you know?"

DISCUSSION

Which is Greatest?

15 MIN   CLASS

Math Focus Points for Discussion

◆ Ordering decimals and justifying their order through reasoning about decimal representations, equivalents, and relationships

Write the following decimal numbers on the board:

0.125   0.25   0.02   0.3

Ask students to put the four numbers in order from least to greatest and to write how they figured out the correct order.① When they finish, they share their thinking with a partner. Copies of Decimal Grids (M14) should be available. Students will not necessarily actually shade in the amounts represented by each decimal, but they can use these grids to help them visualize each quantity. Some students may want to shade them in as well.

After a few minutes, ask students to explain their thinking.

Students might say:

 "I know 0.02 is the smallest because there's a 0 in the tenths place, 0.3 is the largest because there's a 3 in the tenths place, so 0.125 and 0.25 are in the middle!"

 "I know 0.02 is the smallest—that's two hundredths so it's tiny. I know that 0.125 is $\frac{1}{8}$, that's $12\frac{1}{2}$%, and 0.25 is the same as 25%, that comes next, then 0.3 is 30%, so it's the largest."

 "I pictured them on the hundredths grid. 0.02 only fills up two squares, 0.125 fills up $12\frac{1}{2}$ squares, 0.25 fills up 25 squares, and 0.3 fills up 30 squares."

Ask questions that focus on visualizing how 0.125 relates to the other numbers.

How did you know that 125 thousandths is the same as $12\frac{1}{2}$ hundredths? . . . If I look at 0.125 and 0.3, there's a way in which 0.125 looks larger; after all, 125 is much greater than 3. How can you convince me that 0.125 is actually smaller than 0.3?

Encourage students to use images of the decimal grids or of the number line to justify their responses.

2 Decimals In Between Game

30 MIN   CLASS   PAIRS

Decimals In Between is a new activity, although students played a similar game in Unit 4. Have available copies of *Decimals In Between* (M15).

Before introducing the game, give students a few minutes to look at Decimal Cards, Set B (M13). Ask students to find the least and greatest numbers in this set *(0.025 and 0.975)* and to say what they are and what they know about them (e.g., 0.025 is two hundredths and five thousandths, 0.975 is close to 1). Ask what they notice about this set as a whole. Students generally notice that these cards are all thousandths, that there are no equivalent decimals, and that they all end in 5. You may want to ask students what the 5 means in all of these numbers (e.g., that each number is composed of some number of hundredths plus 5 thousandths or that each number is some number of hundredths plus $\frac{1}{2}$ of a hundredth).❷

Spend a few minutes reviewing with students how this game is played.

Who remembers playing the *In Between Game* when we were studying fractions? We're going to play a new version of this game, using the Decimal Cards. You start by laying out the three "landmark" cards, 0, $\frac{1}{2}$, and 1. Otherwise, all of the rules are the same. Remember that the object of the game is to place Decimal Cards in order from 0 to 1. The person who plays all or most of his or her cards is the winner.

To remind students of the game, show the drawing you made on the chart paper or on a transparency:

| 0 | 0.075 | 0.275 | | 0.425 | $\frac{1}{2}$ | 0.555 | 0.625 | | 1 |

Let's say that a game is in progress, and this is how the game looks right now. These five cards have been played. Remember that you can't move cards that already have edges touching. Let's say I want to play the 0.35 card. What landmark is 35 hundredths close to? ($\frac{1}{2}$) Is it more or less than $\frac{1}{2}$? How do you know? . . . Can I play this card? Is it more or less than 0.425? How do you know? . . . Is it more or less than 0.275? How do you know?

Teaching Note

❷ **Decimal Cards Layout** On a blank transparency or whiteboard, draw three groups of Decimal Cards from left to right: group one—0, 0.075, 0.275; group two—0.425, $\frac{1}{2}$, 0.555, 0.625; group three—1. Leave space in between the groups of Decimal Cards, so that you can place the Decimal Cards that you draw between these groups when playing an introductory round of *Decimals In Between* with the class.

▲ Resource Masters, M15

When students agree, place the 0.35 card to the left of the 0.425 card. If you think it is necessary, draw another one or two cards and ask students to help you decide where to play them.

Remind students to find and lay out the cards labeled 0, $\frac{1}{2}$, and 1 before they start and to jot down their scores after each round.

ONGOING ASSESSMENT: Observing Students at Work

Students compare and order decimals.

- **Are students able to order decimals correctly?** Are they able to use place-value clues to help them (e.g., 0.2 is larger than 0.125 because two tenths is larger than one tenth)?

- **Can students read and interpret decimals in the thousandths?** Do they know whether a decimal number is close to 0, $\frac{1}{2}$, or 1?

- **What other strategies do students use for comparing decimals?** Do they consider fraction and percent equivalents? Do they use the hundredths and thousandths grids to help them visualize the decimals?

As you observe students playing, encourage them to check each other's moves.

As students become more comfortable playing the game, help them develop strategies for playing the game. Ask questions to help them consider more than one card at a time.

- Where is a good place to play that card? Does that allow you to place other cards that you have in later moves, or does it limit what you can do?

- If you play that card, does that block any of the other player's cards?

DIFFERENTIATION: Supporting the Range of Learners

Intervention If some students do not feel ready to start playing on their own, you can play with a small group. You act as the first player and the group of students can collaborate as the second player. Students who are just beginning to develop an understanding of thousandths and are too unsure of the meaning of these numbers to play the game, yet can work in pairs to put all the Decimal Cards (Sets A and B) in order, or they can draw a subset of cards (perhaps 10–12 cards) to put in order. They can use the Decimal Grids (M14) to visualize or shade in the numbers on the cards.

Students who are still developing an understanding of hundredths can play the game with Set A of the Decimal Cards and may want to start with only four cards each. These students could also simply draw five of the Decimal Cards and put them in order. Encourage students to use Hundredths Grids (M12) to help them compare decimals.

Extension Students who easily play at least five rounds (a complete game) and have no difficulty comparing and ordering the decimals can work in pairs to put all the Decimal Cards in order (Sets A and B together) and see whether they can find a pattern to their order. *(They start with 0.025 and increase by 0.025.)*

DISCUSSION
3 Comparing Decimals

15 MIN   CLASS

Math Focus Points for Discussion

◆ Ordering decimals and justifying their order through reasoning about decimal representations, equivalents, and relationships

Students have now been using the Decimal Cards for two sessions. To give students practice in approximating unfamiliar decimal fractions, ask students for examples of decimal numbers less than one that are not on the decimal cards.

If we look at our Decimal Cards, are those the only decimals between 0 and 1? Who can give me an example of a decimal that is larger than 0.5 and smaller than 0.525?

Give students a moment to think about this and discuss it with a partner. They can look at a thousandths grid to help them think about the question. Collect some answers, and ask students how they figured them out. Encourage students to use fraction equivalents and to refer to the decimal grids to help them explain their answers.

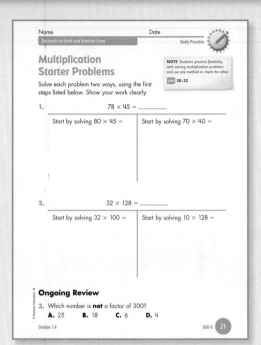

▲ Student Activity Book, p. 21

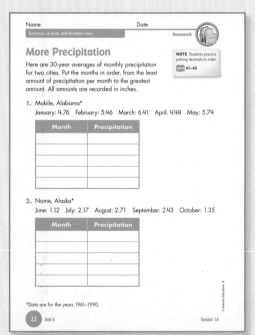

▲ Student Activity Book, p. 22

Students might say:

 "I thought of $\frac{1}{2}$ as 500 thousandths because 500 is $\frac{1}{2}$ of 1,000. Then it was easier to figure out, because in between 500 thousandths and 525 thousandths, there's 501, 502, 503, and you can keep going."

 "Five tenths is like 50 hundredths, and 0.525 is a little more than 52 hundredths, so 51 hundredths has to be between them."

A few students may think about decimal fractions that are smaller than thousandths.

Students might say:

 "You can do 0.5001 or 0.50001 or 0.500001. You can just keep going forever making smaller and smaller parts."

Write on the board two more pairs of numbers and ask students to find numbers that are between them.

$$0.925 \text{ and } 0.95 \qquad 0 \text{ and } 0.025$$

This time ask each student to write numbers individually, and then share with a partner. Finally, share some of the responses and justifications with the whole class.

SESSION FOLLOW-UP

Daily Practice and Homework

 Daily Practice: For ongoing review, have students complete *Student Activity Book* page 21.

 Homework: Students practice putting decimals in order on *Student Activity Book* page 22.

Student Math Handbook: Students and families may use *Student Math Handbook* pages 61–62 and G5 for reference and review. See pages 147–151 in the back of this unit.

Assessment: Decimal Problems

Math Focus Points

◆ Representing decimal fractions as parts of an area

◆ Identifying decimal, fraction, and percent equivalents

◆ Ordering decimals and justifying their order through reasoning about decimal representations, equivalents, and relationships

Today's Plan		Materials
① ACTIVITY **Introducing *Smaller to Larger***	15 MIN CLASS PAIRS	• M11; M13; M16*
② MATH WORKSHOP **Comparing Decimals** **2A** *Smaller to Larger* **2B** *Decimals In Between* **2C** Assessment: Decimal Problems	45 MIN	**2A** • M11; M13; M16* **2B** • M11–13; M15 **2C** • *Student Activity Book,* pp. 23–25 • M12; M17*; M18* ☑
③ SESSION FOLLOW-UP **Daily Practice and Homework**		• *Student Activity Book,* pp. 26–27 • *Student Math Handbook,* pp. 54, 55–56, 61–62

*See *Materials to Prepare,* p. 21.

Ten-Minute Math

Estimation and Number Sense Using Digit Cards, create two, 3-digit by 1-digit multiplication problems (__ __ __ × __). Give students 30 seconds to mentally estimate a product as close as possible to the exact answer. Students may jot down partial products if they wish. Some students may be able to determine the exact answer. Have two or three students explain their work, and record these strategies on the board or overhead.

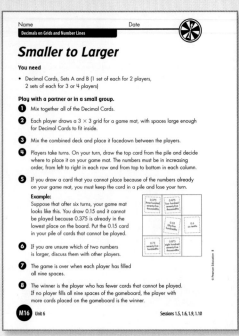

▲ **Resource Masters, M16**

15 MIN CLASS PAIRS

ACTIVITY

1 Introducing *Smaller to Larger*

To introduce the game, demonstrate at the board or overhead. Students can refer to copies of *Smaller to Larger* (M16).

Draw a 3 × 3 grid (like a large tic-tac-toe board) to use as the game board. Explain to students the basic rules of the game.

The goal of this game is to fill all of the spaces on the game board with decimal cards. The numbers must be placed in increasing order (least to greatest) from left to right in each row and in increasing order from top to bottom in each column. After a card has been played, it cannot be moved. When you play the game on your own, you'll each draw your own game board and take turns drawing cards from the deck and playing on your own board.

Draw a Decimal Card (M11, M13) and have students decide where it should be played, reading each decimal as the card is played. In the following example, five cards have been played, and the next card picked is 0.85.

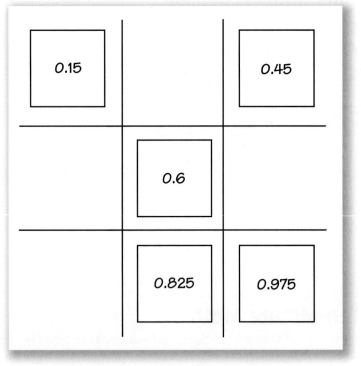

Talk to your neighbor about where we could play the 85 hundredths card.

Stuart says that we can't play the card because in the bottom row we already played 825 thousandths and 975 thousandths and this card goes in between them. Are there any comments? Shandra disagrees. She says that we could play it in the last spot in the middle row because it's greater than 6 tenths and goes between 45 hundredths and 975 thousandths in the last column. Are there any comments? Shandra is right; we can play the card there. Remember the rules; the decimals have to be in order from left to right and top to bottom, but it's all right if the last card in one row is bigger than a card in the first one or two spaces of the row below.

Play the rest of the game with the class, filling up all nine spaces.

MATH WORKSHOP

45 MIN

② Comparing Decimals

Introduce the Math Workshop by letting students know that they will spend the rest of this session and the next one playing decimal games and working on some decimal problems. The problems on *Student Activity Book* pages 23–25 are used to assess students on representing and ordering decimals.

Decide who is ready to start playing *Smaller to Larger* on their own, who should first play in a small group with you, and who might benefit from continuing to play *Decimals In Between*. *Smaller to Larger* is a more difficult game than *Decimals In Between*. Students who are unsure about the meaning of hundredths and thousandths can play more rounds of *Decimals In Between* or one of the variations suggested in Session 1.4.

Although you will get some information from students' completed papers for the assessment, you will learn more from interacting with students as they are working on the problems. During today's session, you can identify some students who understand how to play *Smaller to Larger* well and would be good teachers for other students so that you can be free to observe during Session 1.6.

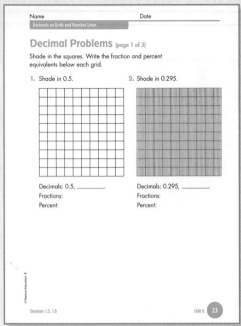

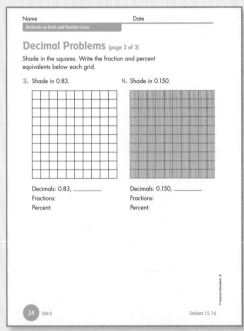

▲ Student Activity Book, p. 24 PORTFOLIO

2A *Smaller to Larger*

PAIRS

Students compare and order decimals while considering the advantages and disadvantages of placing numbers in certain positions on the game board.

Playing Smaller to Larger *challenges students to rely on their understanding of place value to order decimals.*

ONGOING ASSESSMENT: Observing Students at Work

Students place, compare, and order decimals on a game board.

- **Are students able to order decimals correctly?** Are they able to use place-value clues to help them (e.g., 0.2 is greater than 0.125 because two tenths is greater than one tenth)?

- **Can students read and interpret decimals in the thousandths?** Do they know whether a decimal number is close to 0, $\frac{1}{2}$, or 1?

- **What other strategies do students use for comparing decimals?** Do they consider fraction and percent equivalents? Do they use or visualize hundredths and thousandths grids?

- **What strategies are students using for placing cards on the gameboard?** Do they put cards in places that leave openings for placing further cards? Or do they put them in places that make it impossible to move?

As students are playing the game, ask questions to help them consider which card to play and where to play it.

- What could you play in this space? Would it have to be greater than $\frac{1}{2}$ [$0, \frac{1}{4}, \frac{3}{4}$] or less than $\frac{1}{2}$ [$\frac{1}{4}, \frac{3}{4}, 1$]?

- Where is a good place to play that card? Does that allow you to place other cards that you have in later moves? Or does it limit what you can do in your next moves?

- If you played that card there [point to a specific location on the board], will you still be able to play your other cards?

DIFFERENTIATION: Supporting the Range of Learners

Intervention Some students who are playing *Smaller to Larger* may still have difficulty getting started playing this game because it is more difficult to keep track of the rules and the values of the numbers and to think through strategy all at the same time. Some students may find it more comfortable to get used to the rules of this game while playing with only Set A of the Decimal Cards. When they are used to the rules, Set B can be added.

2B Decimals In Between

PAIRS

For a complete description, see Session 1.4, page 45.

2C Assessment: Decimal Problems

INDIVIDUALS

Students shade in parts of a square represented by a decimal fraction and solve problems that involve comparing decimal fractions in tenths, hundredths, and thousandths.

Make sure that copies of Hundredths Grids (M12) and Thousandths Grids (M17) are available for students as they solve the problems on *Student Activity Book* page 25.

This assessment addresses Benchmarks 1 and 2 for this unit. (Benchmark 1: Read, write, and interpret decimal fractions to thousandths. Benchmark 2: Order decimals to the thousandths.)

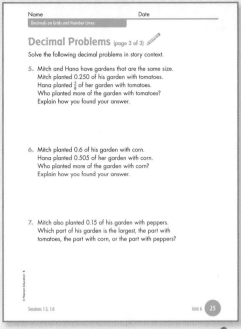

Decimal Problems (page 3 of 3)

Solve the following decimal problems in story context.

5. Mitch and Hana have gardens that are the same size. Mitch planted 0.250 of his garden with tomatoes. Hana planted $\frac{3}{8}$ of her garden with tomatoes. Who planted more of the garden with tomatoes? Explain how you found your answer.

6. Mitch planted 0.6 of his garden with corn. Hana planted 0.505 of her garden with corn. Who planted more of the garden with corn? Explain how you found your answer.

7. Mitch also planted 0.15 of his garden with peppers. Which part of his garden is the largest, the part with tomatoes, the part with corn, or the part with peppers?

▲ **Student Activity Book, p. 25**

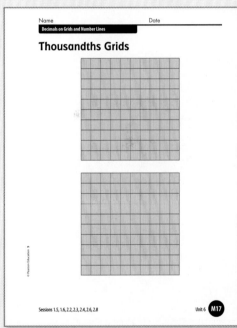

Thousandths Grids

▲ **Resource Masters, M17; T66**

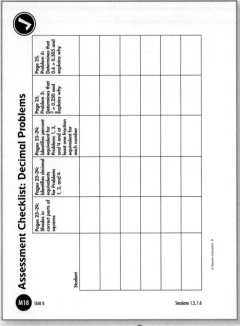

Note that students will make some different choices about how many equivalents they write for each type of number (decimals, fractions, percents) on *Student Activity Book* pages 23–24. However, every student should show somewhere on this page that they know how to determine tenths, hundredths, and thousandths equivalents in both fraction and decimal form. If you do not see evidence of this, ask students to think about other equivalents.

What would 150 thousandths look like if you represented it on a hundredths grid? I'd like you to try that and see whether you can come up with any other decimals and fractions equivalent to 150 thousandths.

Encourage students to use hundredths and thousandths grids to solve the problems on *Student Activity Book* page 25.

Keep track of students' responses on copies of Assessment Checklist: Decimal Problems (M18). Each checklist has room to record observations for six students. The checklist focuses on particular problems and parts of problems for this assessment.

ONGOING ASSESSMENT: Observing Students at Work

Students shade in parts of squares to represent decimal fractions. They solve problems comparing fractions and decimals.

- **Can students read and interpret decimal notation that represents tenths, hundredths, and thousandths?**

- **Can students determine fraction, decimal, and percent equivalents?** In particular, do they know how to find and interpret hundredths and thousandths equivalents for tenths (e.g., 0.5 = 0.50 = 0.500)?

- **Do they recognize common equivalents (e.g., 0.250 = $\frac{1}{4}$, 0.125 = $\frac{1}{8}$)?**

- **Can they compare decimal fractions that have different numbers of places; in other words, tenths with hundredths, hundredths with thousandths (e.g., Which is more, 0.6 or 0.505?)?**

DIFFERENTIATION: Supporting the Range of Learners

Intervention Finding the percent for 0.295 is particularly challenging. Not all students are expected to know that the percent equivalent is 29.5% or $29\frac{1}{2}$%. Ask students who are having difficulty with this problem to represent this decimal on a hundredths grid and to think about how many hundredths are equivalent to 0.295.

Extension Students who easily complete the problems on *Student Activity Book* page 25 can solve this additional problem:

Hana decides to plant the rest of her garden with pumpkins. How much of her garden did she plant with pumpkins?

SESSION FOLLOW-UP

3 Daily Practice and Homework

 Daily Practice: For reinforcement of this unit's content, have students complete *Student Activity Book* page 26.

 Homework: Students practice ordering decimals by using information from the 2004 swimming U.S. Summer National Championships on *Student Activity Book* page 27. Times are recorded in seconds; 56.75 means 56 and 75 hundredths seconds. (Note: For Problem 2, there is a tie (50.54) for 4th and 5th places. Students may point out that these two people would tie for fourth and there would be no fifth place.)

 Student Math Handbook: Students and families may use *Student Math Handbook* pages 54, 55–56, 61–62 for reference and review. See pages 147–151 in the back of this unit.

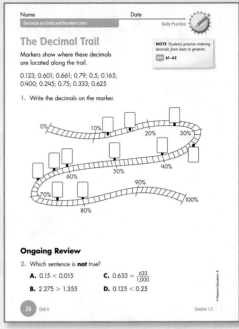

▲ Student Activity Book, p. 26

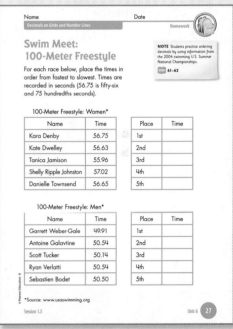

▲ Student Activity Book, p. 27

Ordering Decimals

Math Focus Points

◆ Representing decimal fractions as parts of an area

◆ Identifying decimal, fraction, and percent equivalents

◆ Ordering decimals and justifying their order through reasoning about decimal representations, equivalents, and relationships

Today's Plan		Materials
MATH WORKSHOP **① Comparing Decimals** **1A** *Smaller to Larger* **1B** *Decimals In Between* **1C** Assessment: Decimal Problems	🕐 60 MIN	**1A** • M11; M13; M16 **1B** • M11–M13; M15 **1C** • *Student Activity Book,* pp. 23–25 • M12; M17; M18
SESSION FOLLOW-UP **② Daily Practice and Homework**		• *Student Activity Book,* pp. 29–30 • *Student Math Handbook,* pp. 61–62; G14, G5

Ten-Minute Math

Estimation and Number Sense Using Digit Cards, create two 3-digit by 1-digit multiplication problems (___ ___ ___ × ___). Give students 30 seconds to mentally estimate a product as close as possible to the exact answer. Students may jot down partial products if they wish. Some students may be able to determine the exact answer. Have two or three students explain their work, and record these strategies on the board or overhead.

MATH WORKSHOP

① Comparing Decimals

60 MIN

From your observations in the last session, decide whether there are additional students who are ready to start playing *Smaller to Larger* on their own or who should first play in a small group with you or with another student who understands the game well.

Make sure that all students finish the problems on *Student Activity Book* pages 23–25 for the assessment.

1A *Smaller to Larger*

PAIRS

For a complete description see Session 1.5, pages 50–51.

1B *Decimals In Between*

PAIRS

For a complete description see Session 1.4, pages 45–46.

Playing Decimals In Between *helps students establish relationships between various decimals and "landmark" numbers such as 0, $\frac{1}{2}$ and 1.*

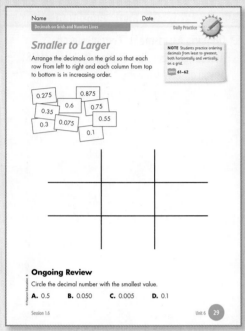

▲ Student Activity Book, p. 29

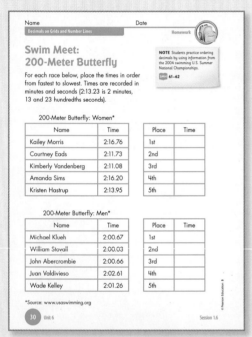

▲ Student Activity Book, p. 30

1C Assessment: Decimal Problems

For a complete description see Session 1.5, pages 53–54.

SESSION FOLLOW-UP
Daily Practice and Homework

 Daily Practice: For reinforcement of this unit's content, have students complete *Student Activity Book* page 29.

 Homework: Students practice ordering decimals by using information from the 2004 swimming U.S. Summer National Championships on *Student Activity Book* page 30. Times are recorded in minutes and seconds and look like this: 2:13.23, which means 2 minutes, 13 and 23 hundredths seconds. You may want to point out this notation to students. It is frequently used to report times like this for sporting events.

Student Math Handbook: Students and families may use *Student Math Handbook* pages 61–62 and G14, G5 for reference and review. See pages 147–151 in the back of this unit.

Fractions as Division

Math Focus Points

◆ Interpreting fractions as division

◆ Identifying everyday uses of fractions and decimals

◆ Identifying decimal, fraction, and percent equivalents

Vocabulary

numerator
denominator

Today's Plan		Materials
① DISCUSSION **Fractions to Decimals on the Calculator**	20 MIN CLASS PAIRS	• Calculators
② ACTIVITY **Win/Loss Records**	40 MIN CLASS INDIVIDUALS	• *Student Activity Book,* p. 31 • Chart: "Win/Loss Records"* • Calculators
③ SESSION FOLLOW-UP **Daily Practice and Homework**		• *Student Activity Book,* pp. 32–33 • *Student Math Handbook,* pp. 59–60

*See *Materials to Prepare,* p. 23.

Ten-Minute Math

Estimation and Number Sense Using Digit Cards, create two 3-digit divided by 1-digit division problems (__ __ __ ÷ __). Give students 30 seconds to mentally estimate a quotient as close as possible to the exact answer. Students may jot down partial products or quotients if they wish. Some students may be able to determine the exact answer. Have two or three students explain their work, and record these strategies on the board or overhead.

DISCUSSION

Fractions to Decimals on the Calculator

20 MIN CLASS PAIRS

Math Focus Points for Discussion

◆ Interpreting fractions as division

◆ Identifying decimal and fraction equivalents

All students need access to a calculator during this discussion. Write these fractions on the board:

$$\frac{1}{2} \qquad \frac{1}{4}$$

Let's say that I want to find the equivalent decimals for these fractions, and I don't know what they are. Who knows how I could use a calculator to find out? Try it.

Give students a few minutes to work with the calculator and then collect students' ideas. If necessary, explain to students that one way to think of a fraction is as division. The line is a division sign: $\frac{1}{2}$ represents 1 divided by 2 and $\frac{1}{4}$ represents 1 divided by 4. Doing the division on the calculator gives the decimal equivalent on the display.

Terrence tells us that if we divide 1 by 2 on the calculator, we get 0.5 on the display. What other numbers could you divide to get 0.5?

Give students a minute or so to work with a partner to write some division expressions that are equivalent to 0.5. Collect students' answers and write them on the board with a division sign and as a fraction:

0.5

1 ÷ 2 $\frac{1}{2}$

2 ÷ 4 $\frac{2}{4}$

3 ÷ 6 $\frac{3}{6}$

50 ÷ 100 $\frac{50}{100}$

200 ÷ 400 $\frac{200}{400}$

Ask students why they think this is true, using some of their examples.

I've heard some people say, "You can't divide a smaller number by a larger number," but that's what you have just done. What do you think about that statement? When you divide 1 by 2 or 2 by 4 or 50 by 100, you always get 5 tenths. Why do you think this happens?

Students may never have thought about fractions as division before and may not be articulate about why dividing the numerator of a fraction such as $\frac{1}{2}$, $\frac{2}{4}$, or $\frac{3}{6}$ by its denominator results in 0.5. Encourage students to try to articulate their ideas. If students need some help in formulating their thoughts, remind them of what they know about division.

What two numbers could you divide on the calculator to get a quotient of 2? . . . Try a few. . . . How did you know that when you divided 50 by 25 or 200 by 100, you'd get 2? . . . Can you use the same kind of idea to explain why 25 divided by 50 or 100 divided by 200 is 0.5?

Putting this division in a context may also be useful.

If you have 50 brownies to divide equally among 25 people, how many brownies does each person get? If you have 25 brownies to divide equally among 50 people, how many brownies does each person get?

Repeat this activity for $\frac{1}{4}$.

What numbers can you divide on your calculators so that 0.25 shows up in the display?

Let students work with the calculator and then collect some of their ideas.

0.25

$1 \div 4$	$\frac{1}{4}$
$2 \div 8$	$\frac{2}{8}$
$3 \div 12$	$\frac{3}{12}$
$50 \div 200$	$\frac{50}{200}$
$200 \div 800$	$\frac{200}{800}$

ACTIVITY
2 Win/Loss Records

Show students the chart you made of win/loss statistics.

Teams:	W	L	Record
Dragons	29	11	0.725
Vikings	26	13	0.667
Falcons	21	17	0.553
Eagles	19	19	0.500
Bears	12	26	0.316

Here's a list of some middle-school basketball teams and the number of games they won and lost for one year. Look at this list with a partner. How do you think the decimals in the last column were computed? What do you think they mean? Look at their relationship to the wins and losses.

Give students a few minutes to talk with a partner and to experiment with a calculator to see whether they can interpret the last column and figure out how it is computed. Gather students' ideas. Some students may know about sports records such as this one and be able to interpret them. Others may recognize that the team with equal wins and losses has a record of 0.500, that teams with more wins than losses have records greater than $\frac{1}{2}$, and that teams with more losses than wins have records less than $\frac{1}{2}$.

As students bring up the need to compute the total number of games played, add an additional column to the chart showing this information (or, if students seem stuck, suggest adding this piece of information yourself).

Margaret says that to find the decimal, you have to know the total number of games played, and she figured it out for the Dragons by adding 29 and 11. The Dragons have won 29 games out of 40 games played, so she divided 29 by 40 and got 0.725.

On the board, write $\frac{29}{40} = 0.725$.

Just as you found the decimal for $\frac{1}{2}$ and $\frac{1}{4}$ by dividing the numerator by the denominator, Margaret created the fraction $\frac{29}{40}$ for 29 out of 40 games and then divided to find the decimal 0.725. What familiar fraction or percent is 0.725 close to? If you were reporting how many of their games the Dragons won, what familiar fraction or percent could you use?

Students might say:

"725 is close to 72 hundredths—that's a little under 75 hundredths, which is the same as $\frac{3}{4}$."

"725 is like 72 and a half hundredths, which is the same as $72\frac{1}{2}\%$. They won a little more than 70% of their games."

Give students a few minutes to experiment with how to find the rest of the winning records on the calculator. As students are working on this, ask them to think about how to write the winning records as percents.

Add columns to the chart, and ask students to help you write the fractions and percents for the teams' records.

Teams:	W	L	Record	Fraction	Percent
Dragons	29	11	0.725	$\frac{29}{40}$	73%
Vikings	26	13	0.667	$\frac{26}{39}$	67%
Falcons	21	17	0.553	$\frac{21}{38}$	55%
Eagles	19	19	0.500	$\frac{19}{38}$	50%
Bears	12	26	0.316	$\frac{12}{38}$	32%

Ask students what they noticed or what questions they have. The following three key ideas should emerge:

- The display on the calculator shows more numbers (places) than the chart. Numbers are rounded off to thousandths. (Decimals that fill the calculator display are discussed in Session 1.8.)

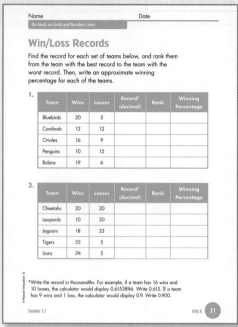

▲ Student Activity Book, p. 31

- *Percent* means "hundredths." Students should know that $0.500 = 50\%$, but they are not experienced with finding percent equivalents for thousandths. Encourage them to think about how many hundredths are in each decimal; for example, they may say that 0.667 is between 66% and 67%. Students may remember from their fractions work that this is very close to $\frac{2}{3}$, or $66\frac{2}{3}$. Other students may be able to visualize what 0.667 would look like on a thousandths grid and explain that it is 66 and $\frac{7}{10}$ hundredths or 66.7%. Accept what students offer for this column, (e.g., for the Dragons' record, they might suggest 72% (truncating the number), 73% (rounding up), "between 72% and 73%," or 72.5%).

- One reason to use decimals or percents to compare instead of fractions is that it is much easier to compare and order these numbers. For example, it is easier to compare 0.725 and 0.667 than to compare $\frac{29}{40}$ and $\frac{26}{39}$ because the decimals are both in terms of thousandths.

Keep in mind that the purpose of this activity is to help students understand what decimals are, what their relationship to fractions is, and how they can be used, and not necessarily having students become proficient in finding and comparing records.

Students use the remainder of the session to complete *Student Activity Book* page 31.

ONGOING ASSESSMENT: Observing Students at Work

Students use a calculator to find a decimal equivalent to a fraction that represents number of wins out of total games played.

- **Do students understand how to find the decimal equivalent for a fraction on the calculator?**

- **Are students able to make sense of what the display on the calculator shows?** Are they able to write the decimal using three places, either by truncating or rounding?

- **Can students put the decimal representations for the records in order?** Can they find an approximate percentage for each decimal fraction?

Remind students that the winning record is the number of wins out of the total number of games. Help students find approximate percent equivalents for the less familiar decimals such as 0.871795 (for the Lions' record, $\frac{34}{39}$). Remind them to look at how many hundredths are in this number.

DIFFERENTIATION: Supporting the Range of Learners

Intervention If some students are having difficulty remembering to find the total number of games, suggest that they create two additional columns on another sheet of paper, one for the total number of games and one for the fraction that represents number of wins out of total games.

SESSION FOLLOW-UP

3 Daily Practice and Homework

 Daily Practice: For ongoing review, have students complete *Student Activity Book* page 32.

 Homework: Students use information from the 2004 U.S. Summer Nationals to practice ordering decimals on *Student Activity Book* page 33. (There is a tie for fourth place, 26.19 seconds, in the women's competition.)

 Student Math Handbook: Students and families may use *Student Math Handbook* pages 59–60 for reference and review. See pages 147–151 in the back of this unit.

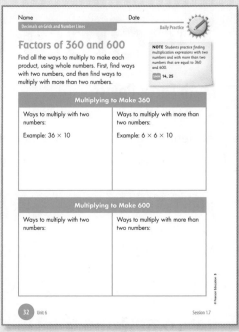

▲ **Student Activity Book, p. 32**

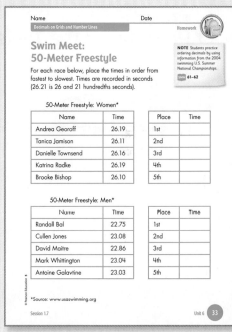

▲ **Student Activity Book, p. 33**

Decimal Equivalents

Math Focus Points

- ◆ Interpreting fractions as division
- ◆ Identifying decimal and fraction equivalents
- ◆ Interpreting the meaning of digits in a decimal number

Vocabulary

repeating decimal

Today's Plan

	Materials
ACTIVITY **① Introducing the Division Table** 15 MIN CLASS PAIRS	• *Student Activity Book*, p. 35 • T67 ; T65 • Calculators
ACTIVITY **② Completing the Division Table** 35 MIN INDIVIDUALS PAIRS	• *Student Activity Book*, p. 35 • M12 • Calculators
DISCUSSION **③ Patterns on the Table** 10 MIN CLASS	• *Student Activity Book*, p. 35
SESSION FOLLOW-UP **④ Daily Practice**	• *Student Activity Book*, p. 36 • *Student Math Handbook*, pp. 59–60

Ten-Minute Math

Estimation and Number Sense Using Digit Cards, create two 3-digit divided by 1-digit division problems (___ ___ ___ ÷ ___). Give students 30 seconds to mentally estimate a quotient as close as possible to the exact answer. Students may jot down partial products or quotients if they wish. Some students may be able to determine the exact answer. Have two or three students explain their work, and record these strategies on the board or overhead.

ACTIVITY

Introducing the Division Table

15 MIN · CLASS · PAIRS

In this activity, students create a table that organizes the fractions they worked with in Unit 4, as well as sevenths, ninths, and elevenths, and their decimal equivalents. The following two important mathematical ideas are developed in filling out the table:

- Fractions are a way to notate division. When the numerator is divided by the denominator, the result is an equivalent decimal. If the numerator and denominator of a fraction are both whole numbers greater than 0 and the numerator is a multiple of the denominator, division results in a whole number (e.g., $\frac{6}{3} = 2$, $\frac{4}{4} = 1$). Otherwise, the division results in a number with a decimal portion (e.g., $\frac{1}{4} = 0.25$, $\frac{9}{4} = 2.25$).

- Students can use fraction and percent equivalents learned in Unit 4 to determine decimal equivalents (e.g., $\frac{1}{4}$, $\frac{2}{8}$, and $\frac{3}{12}$ are equivalent, so each equals 0.25).

Students should be able to fill in most of the chart from their work in Unit 4. Students begin the task in this session by finding the decimal equivalents for halves, thirds, fourths, fifths, sixths, eighths, tenths, and twelfths. They complete the table in the Math Workshop in Sessions 1.9 and 1.10.

To introduce this activity, show the transparency of Fraction-to-Decimal Division Table (T67).

This is a division table. It is similar to a multiplication table: the numbers we are going to divide are shown across the top and down the left side, and the answers are recorded in the boxes. We're going to use this division table to record decimal equivalents for fractions. The numbers in the top row represent the numerators of fractions. The numbers in the left column are the denominators.

Point to a few different cells inside the table—for example, $\frac{4}{5}$, $\frac{6}{3}$, and $\frac{9}{12}$ —and ask what fraction is being represented. Also point to one row of cells, 8 for example, and make certain that students realize that all decimals in that row will be equivalent to eighths.

Now students can look at their own table on *Student Activity Book* page 35. Point to the cell for $\frac{1}{2}$, and have students identify which fraction is represented.

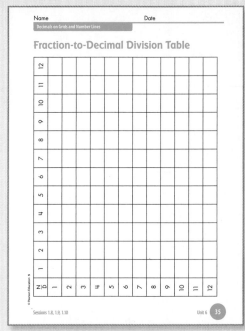

▲ **Student Activity Book, p. 35; Resource Masters, M19; T67**

We're going to write the decimal equivalents in these boxes. What decimal is equivalent to $\frac{1}{2}$? Write 0.5 in the box. Talk to a neighbor—where else on this table will you write 0.5 for a fraction that is equivalent to $\frac{1}{2}$? When you and your partner agree, write 0.5 in the appropriate places. See whether you can find the other five places where 0.5 belongs.

Give students several minutes to do this. Then ask students to name the fractions ($\frac{2}{4}$, $\frac{3}{6}$, $\frac{4}{8}$, $\frac{5}{10}$, $\frac{6}{12}$), and write 0.5 in each of the appropriate cells on the transparency.

$\frac{N}{D}$	1	2	3	4	5	6	7	8	9	10	11	12
1												
2	0.5											
3												
4		0.5										
5												
6			0.5									
7												
8				0.5								
9												
10					0.5							
11												
12						0.5						

It seems like most of you already know several equivalents for $\frac{1}{2}$. As you work, pay attention to the fraction/decimal equivalents you already know and ones you can easily find based on patterns.

Now point to the cell for $\frac{1}{3}$ and ask students what they think the decimal equivalent is for $\frac{1}{3}$.

What happens when you divide 1 by 3? What is the decimal equivalent? What happens when you divide 1 by 3 on the calculator? Can you make sense of the number you see on the calculator display? What is that number? What do you think would happen if more numbers could fit in the calculator display?

Spend a few minutes sharing ideas about the calculator display. Ideas that may come up include these:

- It's a little more than 33 hundredths or 333 thousandths.

- As you move to the right in the number, each 3 represents a smaller and smaller number: 3 tenths, 3 hundredths, 3 thousandths, 3 ten thousandths.

- There are names for these smaller and smaller places, just as there are names for the places to the left of the decimal point. Students may be able to come up with some of these place names by thinking of the sequence for whole numbers: hundred thousandths, millionths, ten millionths, and so on.

Let students know that the decimal equivalent to $\frac{1}{3}$ is a repeating decimal. As you keep dividing, you never get to a final number. Some students may enjoy visualizing how this would work in a context, using the transparency of Decimal Grids (T65).

If you divided a brownie into tenths and you wanted to share it among three people, each person could get three tenths. Then you have one tenth left. Let's say that you divide that into ten hundredths—each person can get three of those hundredths. You have one hundredth left. You divide that into thousandths—how many thousandths in one hundredth? So you have ten thousandths. Again, each person gets three of these tiny pieces and you have one thousandth left.

Some students may begin to see that, because our number system is based on tens, there will always be ten parts to divide up among the three people, with one part that must be divided further.

You will find other repeating decimals as you work. The first number or the second number may be repeated or there may be a pattern of more than one number that repeats. There may be some repeating decimals that you can't tell are repeating decimals because you get only seven digits to the right of the decimal point in your calculator display, and the part that repeats may be longer than that. ❶ ❷

ACTIVITY
❷ Completing the Division Table

35 MIN INDIVIDUALS PAIRS

On *Student Activity Book* page 35, students fill in decimal equivalents for halves, thirds, fourths, fifths, sixths, eighths, tenths, and twelfths. They also fill in the top row of the table. Once they have completed the assignment, they work with a partner to check their answers. ❸

Professional Development

❶ **Teacher Note:** Finding Decimal Equivalents of Fractions by Division, p. 125

Math Notes

❷ **Repeating and Terminating Decimals** As they create the fraction-to-decimal division table, students will notice that thirds, sixths, ninths, elevenths, and twelfths repeat the first or second digits. Sevenths also repeat, but that is not evident from an 8-digit calculator display. Repeating decimals are intriguing to fifth graders, although these sessions are not focused on understanding which fractions result in repeating decimals and why. Encourage students to think about how they know what these decimals mean; for example, how can they tell that the decimal for $\frac{2}{3}$ (truncated on the calculator display as 0.6666666) is less than 0.7? You may want to introduce the notation for repeating decimals. However, remember to caution students that an 8-digit calculator display is often insufficient for determining whether a number is a repeating decimal.

❸ **Truncating and Rounding** Some calculators truncate a repeating decimal. For example, if you carry out the division 2 ÷ 3, the calculator display shows 0.6666666. If you carry out the division 2 ÷ 7, the display shows 0.2857142. Other calculators round up the final digit if the next digit (not shown on the display) would be equal to or greater than 5. For example, the display shows 0.6666667 and 0.2857143 for $\frac{2}{3}$ and $\frac{2}{7}$, respectively. Truncating maintains the repeating decimal pattern, whereas rounding off the last digit may obscure the pattern. If you have calculators that round up, help students understand what is happening in the display.

Professional Development

❹ **Dialogue Box:** Filling in the Fraction-to-Decimal Division Table, p. 140

Let students know that for today they will not be filling in the rows for 7, 9, and 11 (i.e., fractions with these denominators: sevenths, ninths, and elevenths). They may want to circle the 7, 9, and 11 at the beginning of these rows to remind them that they are not working on these rows today. Inform them that the discussion at the end of the session will focus on the patterns they noticed that helped them fill in the table.❹

By creating a Fraction-to-Decimal Division Table, students better understand the relationship between decimals and fractions.

ONGOING ASSESSMENT: Observing Students at Work

Students find decimal equivalents for fractions.

- **Do students start by filling in the decimals they already know?** Which decimal equivalents do they know?

- **What patterns do students notice and use to complete the table (e.g., the row for halves increases by 0.5 each time—0.5, 1, 1.5, 2, 2.5)?**

- **Do they use fraction equivalents (e.g., $\frac{1}{3}$, $\frac{2}{6}$, and $\frac{3}{9}$ are all 0.3333333)?**

- **Do they recognize and fill in the diagonal on the table for fractions equivalent to one?**

As students are working, encourage them to use what they know about fraction and percent equivalents and the patterns that emerge on the chart to fill in the cells. They should fill in as many of the cells as possible without a calculator and then check with you before using a calculator to find others. When you check students' papers, remind them to use equivalents that they know. For example, if students have not filled in $\frac{3}{12}$, ask them what fraction is equivalent to $\frac{3}{12}$. If needed, they can draw a number line divided into twelfths to help them visualize equivalents.

DIFFERENTIATION: Supporting the Range of Learners

Intervention Some students may need to have the scope of the table narrowed for them at first. Identify some parts of the table that you know students can fill in, such as halves, fourths, fifths, and tenths. If they are stuck, they can use the Hundredths Grids (M12) to shade each fraction and then use the grid to determine a decimal equivalent.

Extension Students who easily use fraction equivalents and patterns on the table to complete the work can find the decimal equivalents for sevenths, ninths, and elevenths, using the calculator. Encourage these students to look closely at the decimal equivalents for sevenths to see whether they can determine the pattern that emerges.

DISCUSSION

3 Patterns on the Table

10 MIN CLASS

Math Focus Points for Discussion

◆ Identifying decimal and fraction equivalents

◆ Interpreting the meaning of digits in a decimal number

Even though all students may not be finished completing the table, stop the class to have a brief discussion.

N/D	1	2	3	4	5	6	7	8	9	10	11	12
1	1	2	3	4	5	6	7	8	9	10	11	12
2	0.5	1	1.5	2	2.5	3	3.5	4	4.5	5	5.5	6
3	0.3333	0.666	1	1.333	1.666	2	2.333	2.666	3	3.333	3.66	4
4	0.25	0.5	0.75	1	1.25	1.50	1.75	2	2.25	2.50	2.75	3
5	0.2	0.4	0.6	0.8	1	1.2	1.4	1.6	1.8	2	2.2	2.4
6	0.166	0.333	0.5	0.666	0.8333	1	1.1666	1.333	1.5	1.666	1.8333	2
7							1					
8	0.125	0.25	0.315	0.5	0.625	0.75	0.875	1	1.125	1.25	1.375	1.5
9									1			
10	0.1	0.2	0.3	0.4	0.5	0.6	0.7	0.8	0.9	1	1.1	1.2
11											1	
12	0.08333	0.16666	0.25	0.33333	0.41666	0.5	0.58333	0.666	0.75	0.8333	0.9666	1

Sample Student Work

Professional Development

5 Dialogue Box: Patterns on the Division Table, p. 141

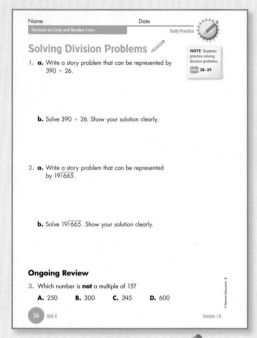

▲ **Student Activity Book, p. 36**

Ask students what patterns they notice on the table, and ask them to think about and explain why some of the patterns they noticed occur. There are many patterns in this table that students may notice but may have no way to explain with what they know about numbers. However, they will enjoy figuring out the pattern. Other patterns are more accessible to them. Focus on the meaning of the decimals, their relationship to familiar decimals, and the meaning of the digits beyond thousandths. Follow up students' observations with questions such as these:

You noticed that the fifths row has a pattern in the tenths: 2, 4, 6, 8, 0. Why do you think this pattern occurs? Why is the decimal for $\frac{1}{5}$ written as 0.2? Why is the decimal for $\frac{2}{5}$ written as 0.4? What is happening as you move across the row? *(the numbers increase by $\frac{1}{5}$ or $\frac{2}{10}$)*

Terrence noticed that there's a diagonal that is all 1s. Why does that happen?

Ask students to look at the table as a whole, not just individual rows and columns. What do they notice?**5**

Let students know that they will have time to complete the table during Math Workshop in the next two sessions.

SESSION FOLLOW-UP
4 Daily Practice

 Daily Practice: For ongoing review, have students complete *Student Activity Book* page 36.

 Student Math Handbook: Students and families may use *Student Math Handbook* pages 59–60 for reference and review. See pages 147–151 in the back of this unit.

Fraction-Decimal Equivalents

Math Focus Points

◆ Ordering decimals and justifying their order through reasoning about decimal representations, equivalents, and relationships

◆ Interpreting fractions as division

◆ Identifying decimal, fraction, and percent equivalents

Today's Plan		Materials
MATH WORKSHOP **① Fraction-Decimal Equivalents** **1A** Fraction-to-Decimal Division Table **1B** Who's Winning? **1C** *Smaller to Larger*	45 MIN	**1A** • *Student Activity Book*, p. 35 • M12 • Calculators **1B** • *Student Activity Book*, p. 37 • Calculators **1C** • M11; M13; M16
DISCUSSION **② Who Has the Best Record?**	15 MIN PAIRS CLASS	• *Student Activity Book*, p. 37 • Chart of wins and losses*
SESSION FOLLOW-UP **③ Daily Practice and Homework**		• *Student Activity Book*, pp. 38–39 • *Student Math Handbook*, pp. 59–60; G14

*See *Materials to Prepare,* p. 23.

Ten-Minute Math

Estimation and Number Sense Using Digit Cards, create 3-digit × 1-digit multiplication problems (__ __ __ × __). Give students 30 seconds to mentally estimate a product as close as possible to the exact answer. Some students may be able to determine the exact answer. Have two or three students explain their work and record these strategies on the board or overhead.

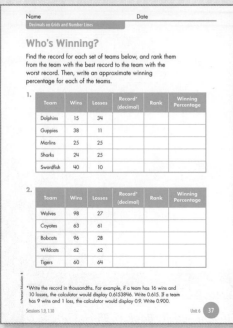

Who's Winning?

Find the record for each set of teams below, and rank them from the team with the best record to the team with the worst record. Then, write an approximate winning percentage for each of the teams.

1.

Team	Wins	Losses	Record* (decimal)	Rank	Winning Percentage
Dolphins	15	34			
Guppies	38	11			
Marlins	25	25			
Sharks	24	25			
Swordfish	40	10			

2.

Team	Wins	Losses	Record* (decimal)	Rank	Winning Percentage
Wolves	98	27			
Coyotes	63	61			
Bobcats	96	28			
Wildcats	62	62			
Tigers	60	64			

*Write the record in thousandths. For example, if a team has 16 wins and 10 losses, the calculator would display 0.6153846. Write 0.615. If a team has 9 wins and 1 loss, the calculator would display 0.9. Write 0.900.

Sessions 1.9, 1.10   Unit 6   37

▲ **Student Activity Book, p. 37**

Fraction-Decimal Equivalents

45 MIN

Students work on three different tasks in this 2-day Math Workshop focused on fraction-decimal equivalents and on comparing decimals. Activity 1B, Who's Winning?, includes more problems like the ones students worked on in Session 1.7 involving win/loss records of teams. Make sure that all students have worked on at least the first problem on *Student Activity Book* page 37 before the discussion at the end of this session.

1A Fraction-to-Decimal Division Table

INDIVIDUALS

See Session 1.8 for a full description of this activity. If students have not already done so, they should complete the rows for 7, 9, and 11 (sevenths, ninths, and elevenths). For these rows, students use calculators to determine the first two or three decimal equivalents. The pattern for ninths ($\frac{1}{9} = 0.111$, $\frac{2}{9} = 0.222$, $\frac{3}{9} = 0.333$) and elevenths ($\frac{1}{11} = 0.0909$, $\frac{2}{11} = 0.1818$, $\frac{3}{11} = 0.2727$) emerges quickly, and students should be able to fill out the rest of the row according to the pattern. The pattern for sevenths is not as easy for students to see. Have them find the first three decimal equivalents with their calculators and ask whether they see any patterns in the numbers. If they have an idea, they can make a guess about what the next number will be and then check it with the calculator. If they need a hint, suggest that they look at the sequence of digits in each decimal. The digits repeat in the same order in each decimal but begin with a different number each time.

Students are not expected to be able to explain or understand all of these patterns, but they have the opportunity to consider and wonder about them. As students are working, focus on asking questions about comparing fractions.

Before you figure out the decimal for $\frac{3}{7}$, approximately what decimal do you expect it to be? Will it be more than 0.5 or less than 0.5? How do you know? What would you estimate the decimal will be? Why?

You found 0.4285714 for $\frac{3}{7}$. Suppose I wanted to say $\frac{3}{7}$ is close to some more familiar decimal number—what number would you choose? $\frac{3}{7}$ is about how much? You found the decimal 0.8333333 for $\frac{5}{6}$. What can you tell me about that number? What more familiar decimals is it in-between? How do you know? What do you think this number would look like if I represented it by shading in a hundredths grid?

ONGOING ASSESSMENT: Observing Students at Work

Students find decimal equivalents for fractions.

- **Do students notice the pattern that emerges for ninths?**
  (The repeating digit is the numerator for $\frac{1}{9}$ through $\frac{8}{9}$.)

- **Do students notice the pattern that emerges for elevenths?**
  (The pair of repeating digits is the numerator multiplied by 9 for $\frac{1}{11}$ through $\frac{10}{11}$.)

- **Are students able to see the pattern that emerges for sevenths?**
  If they do, can they tell how they know which digit to start with in each cell as they move across the row?

DIFFERENTIATION: Supporting the Range of Learners

Extension Students who easily see the patterns that emerge, particularly for ninths and elevenths, should be encouraged to think about what rule they could write for determining what the decimal equivalent would be for any fraction with ninths or elevenths as a denominator. They can also be encouraged to speculate about why the pattern occurs.

1B Who's Winning?

INDIVIDUALS

In this activity, students complete *Student Activity Book* page 37 on which they determine a team's record (number of wins out of total number of events), represented as a decimal. Students then put the set of teams in order from the best record to the worst record.

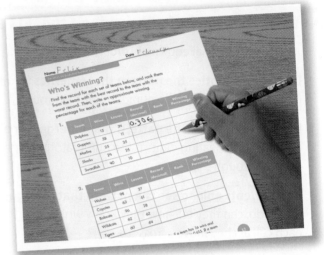

In Who's Winning, students apply their knowledge of decimals to determine sports statistics.

ONGOING ASSESSMENT: Observing Students at Work

Students determine the record for each team by using a calculator and place the teams in order from best to worst.

- **Do students understand how to use the information given in the problem to determine each team's record?**

- **Are students able to make sense of what the display on the calculator shows?** Are they able to write the decimal to three places, either by truncating or rounding?

- **Can students put the decimal representations for the records in order?** Can they find an approximate percentage for each decimal fraction?

DIFFERENTIATION: Supporting the Range of Learners

Intervention If some students are having a hard time remembering to find the total number of games, it may help them organize their work to create two additional columns on another sheet of paper, one for the total number of games and one for the fraction that represents number of wins out of total games.

1C *Smaller to Larger*

INDIVIDUALS PAIRS

For a full description of this activity see Session 1.5, pages 50–51.

DISCUSSION

2 Who Has the Best Record?

15 MIN   PAIRS   CLASS

Math Focus Points for Discussion

◆ Ordering decimals and justifying their order through reasoning about decimal representations, equivalents, and relationships

Post this new set of win/loss records:

Team:	Wins:	Losses:
Bobcats	39	40
Wolves	60	19
Coyotes	41	38
Wildcats	59	19

You've been finding decimals that are equivalent to fractions on *Student Activity Book* pages 35 and 37. Look at the win/loss records for these four teams. Work with a partner, and see whether you can put these teams in order from the best winning record to the worst winning record *without* actually finding the decimal amounts on the calculator. Look at the numbers and think about what you know about fractions and decimals to put the teams in order.

Give students about five minutes to do this task. Some students may not have finished, but bring the group together anyway.

Which team had the best record? *(Wolves)* Who can explain how they figured it out?

Students might say:

"It was easy to compare the Bobcats, Wolves, and Coyotes. They all played 79 games, so the one who won the most games was the Wolves. But we weren't sure what to do about the Wolves and the Wildcats 'cause they're pretty much the same."

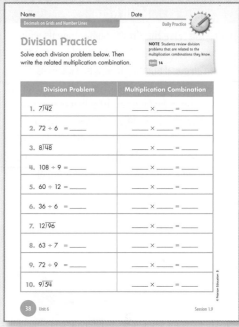

▲ Student Activity Book, p. 38

Math Note

❶ **Playing "Five Hundred"** Some students might know that in some sports, people describe a team with an equal number of wins and losses as having a record of "five hundred." This term is an informal way of referring to the decimal that represents the win percentage, 0.500. Ask students whether they know why the term "five hundred" may be used in this way. For example, if a team has 20 wins and 20 losses, why would that be called a record of "500"?

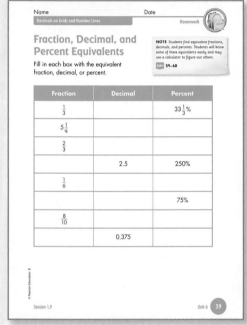

▲ **Student Activity Book, p. 39**

"If the Wildcats had played one more game, they might be the same as the Wolves."

"But we thought that you'd have to say Wolves because the Wolves and Wildcats both lost 19, so that's the same, but the Wolves have more wins."

Which team had the worst record? *(Bobcats)* Who can explain how they figured it out?

Students might say:

"We think it's the Bobcats because they lost 40. That's more than the Coyotes, and they didn't win as many either."

"The Bobcats are really close to 50% losing. We think the Coyotes are close, but not so close."

"The Bobcats are the only team with more losses than wins. Their record has to be less than 50%."❶

SESSION FOLLOW-UP

③ Daily Practice and Homework

Daily Practice: For ongoing review, have students complete *Student Activity Book* page 38.

Homework: Students fill in a chart with fraction, decimal, and percent equivalents on *Student Activity Book* page 39.

Student Math Handbook: Students and families may use *Student Math Handbook* pages 59–60 and G14 for reference and review. See pages 147–151 in the back of this unit.

Assessment: Comparing and Ordering Decimals

Math Focus Points

◆ Ordering decimals and justifying their order through reasoning about decimal representations, equivalents, and relationships

◆ Interpreting fractions as division

◆ Identifying decimal, fraction, and percent equivalents

Today's Plan		Materials
ASSESSMENT ACTIVITY ① **Comparing and Ordering Decimals**	✔ 🕐 👤 15 MIN INDIVIDUALS	• M20*
MATH WORKSHOP ② **Fraction-Decimal Equivalents**	🕐 45 MIN	• *Student Activity Book*, pp. 35, 37 • M11; M12; M13; M16 • Calculators
SESSION FOLLOW-UP ③ **Daily Practice and Homework**		• *Student Activity Book*, pp. 41–42 • *Student Math Handbook*, pp. 59–60, 61–62; G14

*See *Materials to Prepare*, p. 23.

Ten-Minute Math

Practicing Place Value Write 24,305.27 on the board and have students practice saying it. Let students know that this number is read as both "twenty-four thousand three hundred five and twenty-seven hundredths" and as "twenty-four thousand three hundred five point twenty-seven." Ask students:

What is 50 less than 24,305.27? What is 700 more? What is 5,000 less?

Ask students how to write the new number and record it on the board. Then have them compare each sum or difference with 24,305.27. Ask students:

Which places have the same digits? Which do not? Why?

Use 3,710.08 and 59,001.98 to pose more problems.

Professional Development

❶ **Teacher Note:** Assessment: Comparing and Ordering Decimals, p. 127

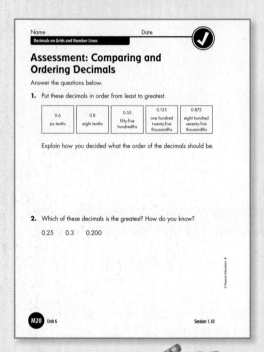

Name _____ **Date** _____

Decimals on Grids and Number Lines ✔

Assessment: Comparing and Ordering Decimals

Answer the questions below.

1. Put these decimals in order from least to greatest.

0.6	0.8	0.55	0.125	0.875
six tenths	eight tenths	fifty-five hundredths	one hundred twenty-five thousandths	eight hundred seventy-five thousandths

Explain how you decided what the order of the decimals should be.

2. Which of these decimals is the greatest? How do you know?

0.25   0.3   0.200

M20 Unit 6   Session 1.10

▲ **Resource Masters, M20**

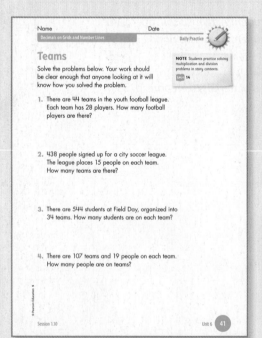

Name _____ **Date** _____

Decimals on Grids and Number Lines   Daily Practice

Teams

Solve the problems below. Your work should be clear enough that anyone looking at it will know how you solved the problem.

NOTE Students practice solving multiplication and division problems in story contexts. Unit 14

1. There are 44 teams in the youth football league. Each team has 28 players. How many football players are there?

2. 438 people signed up for a city soccer league. The league places 15 people on each team. How many teams are there?

3. There are 544 students at Field Day, organized into 34 teams. How many students are on each team?

4. There are 107 teams and 19 people on each team. How many people are on teams?

Session 1.10   Unit 6 41

▲ **Student Activity Book, p. 41**

15 MIN INDIVIDUALS

❶ Comparing and Ordering Decimals

Students complete Assessment: Comparing and Ordering Decimals (M20), which focuses on Benchmark 2: Order decimals to the thousandths. This assessment also assesses students on Benchmark 1: Read, write, and interpret decimal fractions to thousandths.

Remind students that they should explain their answers so that you can understand their thinking about the problems on the assessment. ❶

MATH WORKSHOP

45 MIN

❷ Fraction-Decimal Equivalents

Students continue the Math Workshop started in Session 1.9. For more information, see Session 1.9, pages 74–77.

SESSION FOLLOW-UP

❸ Daily Practice and Homework

Daily Practice: For ongoing review, have students complete *Student Activity Book* page 41.

Homework: Students practice comparing decimals and fractions on *Student Activity Book* page 42.

Student Math Handbook: Students and families may use *Student Math Handbook* pages 59–60, 61–62 and G14 for reference and review. See pages 147–151 in the back of this unit.

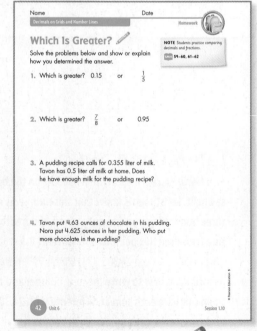

Name _____ **Date** _____

Decimals on Grids and Number Lines   Homework

Which Is Greater?

Solve the problems below and show or explain how you determined the answer.

NOTE Students practice comparing decimals and fractions. Unit 59–60, 61–62

1. Which is greater? 0.15   or $\frac{1}{5}$

2. Which is greater? $\frac{7}{8}$ or   0.95

3. A pudding recipe calls for 0.355 liter of milk. Tavon has 0.5 liter of milk at home. Does he have enough milk for the pudding recipe?

4. Tavon put 4.63 ounces of chocolate in his pudding. Nora put 4.625 ounces in her pudding. Who put more chocolate in the pudding?

42 Unit 6   Session 1.10

▲ **Student Activity Book, p. 42**

Mathematical Emphases

Rational Numbers Understanding the meaning of decimal fractions

Math Focus Points

◆ Representing decimal fractions as parts of an area

Rational Numbers Comparing decimal fractions

Math Focus Points

◆ Ordering decimals and justifying their order through reasoning about decimal representations, equivalents, and relationships

Computation with Rational Numbers Adding decimals

Math Focus Points

◆ Estimating sums of decimal numbers

◆ Using representations to add tenths, hundredths, and thousandths

◆ Adding decimals to the thousandths through reasoning about place value, equivalents, and representations

This Investigation also focuses on

◆ Explaining mathematical reasoning

Adding Decimals

	Student Activity Book	Student Math Handbook	Professional Development: Read Ahead of Time	
SESSION 2.1 p. 86				
Fill Two Students use hundredths grids and Decimal Cards to add decimals. They estimate, solve, and discuss their strategies for adding decimal fractions.	43–44	63–65		
SESSION 2.2 p. 92				
The Jeweler's Gold Students work in groups of three to add numbers that involve tenths, hundredths, and thousandths. They create a poster explaining their solution and discuss and compare strategies.	45–47	63–65	• **Dialogue Box:** Adding Decimals: The Jeweler's Gold, p. 142 • **Teacher Note:** Adding Decimals, p. 132	
SESSION 2.3 p. 97				
Strategies for Adding Decimals Students use Decimal Cards to add tenths, hundredths and thousandths. They consider contexts for adding decimals and discuss and compare different strategies.	49–51	63–65	• **Dialogue Box:** Student Strategies for Adding Decimals, p. 145	
SESSION 2.4 p. 102				
Decimal Problems Students solve addition problems involving decimals to the thousandths. They discuss strategies used for adding decimals and learn a new game, *Decimal Double Compare*.	52–55	63–65; G4		

Materials to Gather	Materials to Prepare
• **M11, Decimal Cards, Set A** (from Session 1.3) • **M13, Decimal Cards, Set B** (from Session 1.3) • **T68, Hundredths Grids for** *Fill Two* 🖥 • **Colored pencils or crayons**	• **M21, Hundredths Grids for** *Fill Two* Make copies for use throughout this Investigation. (more than 2 per student for this session) • **M23,** *Fill Two* Make copies. (as needed)
• **M11, Decimal Cards, Set A** (from Session 1.3; optional) • **M13, Decimal Cards, Set B** (from Session 1.3; optional) • **M12, Hundredths Grids** or **M21, Hundredths Grids for** *Fill Two* (from Sessions 1.3, 2.1; as needed) • **M17, Thousandths Grids** (from Session 1.5; as needed) • **M23,** *Fill Two* (from Session 2.1; optional) • **Large construction paper or chart paper** (1 sheet per group of three) • **Markers**	
• **M11, Decimal Cards, Set A** (from Session 1.3) • **M13, Decimal Cards, Set B** (from Session 1.3) • **M12, Hundredths Grids** or **M21, Hundredths Grids for** *Fill Two* (from Sessions 1.3, 2.1; as needed) • **M17, Thousandths Grids** (from Session 1.5; as needed) • **T68, Hundredths Grids for** *Fill Two* 🖥 (optional)	
• **M11, Decimal Cards, Set A** (from Session 1.3) • **M12, Hundredths Grids** or **M21, Hundredths Grids for** *Fill Two* (from Sessions 1.3, 2.1; as needed) • **M17, Thousandths Grids** (from Session 1.5; as needed) • **M13, Decimal Cards, Set B** (from Session 1.3; optional)	• **M22,** *Decimal Double Compare* Make copies. (as needed)

🖥 Overhead Transparency

Adding Decimals, *continued*

	Student Activity Book	Student Math Handbook	Professional Development: Read Ahead of Time
SESSION 2.5 p. 107			
Decimal Games—Part 1 Students add decimals to the thousandths in the first day of a two-day Math Workshop. They learn a new game, *Close to 1,* in which they add decimals with more than 2 addends.	57–62	63–65; G1, G4	
SESSION 2.6 p. 112			
Decimal Games—Part 2 Students add decimals to the thousandths in the second day of a Math Workshop. They discuss and compare strategies for solving an addition problem.	57, 59–61, 63–64	63–65; G1, G4	
SESSION 2.7 p. 115			
Decimal Games—Part 3 Students add decimals to the thousandths in the third day of a Math Workshop.	57, 59–61, 65	63–65; G1, G4	
SESSION 2.8 p. 117			
End-of-Unit Assessment Students solve two problems as an end of unit assessment, one in which they order decimals and one in which they add decimals.	66	61–62, 63–65	• **Teacher Note:** End-of-Unit Assessment, p. 134

Materials to Gather	Materials to Prepare
• **M11, Decimal Cards, Set A** (from Session 1.3) • **M13, Decimal Cards, Set B** (from Session 1.3) • **M22,** *Decimal Double Compare* (from Session 2.4; as needed) • **M12, Hundredths Grid or M21, Hundredths Grids for** *Fill Two* (from Session 2.1; as needed) • **M23,** *Fill Two* (from Session 2.1; as needed) • **Colored pencils or crayons**	• **M24,** *Close to 1* Make copies. (as needed) • **M25,** *Close to 1* **Recording Sheet** Make copies. (2 per pair plus extras; as needed) • **M26,** *Decimal Double Compare* **Recording Sheet** Make copies. (2 per student plus extras; as needed)
• **M24,** *Close to 1* (from Session 2.5; as needed) • **M25,** *Close to 1* **Recording Sheet** (2 per pair plus extras; from Session 2.5) • **M11, Decimal Cards, Set A** (from Session 1.3) • **M13, Decimal Cards, Set B** (from Session 1.3) • **M12, Hundredths Grids or M21, Hundredths Grids for** *Fill Two* (from Sessions 1.3, 2.1; as needed in class and for homework) • **M22,** *Decimal Double Compare* (from Session 2.4; as needed) • **M26,** *Decimal Double Compare* **Recording Sheet** (2 per student; from Session 2.5) • **M23,** *Fill Two* (from Session 2.1; as needed) • **M17, Thousandths Grids** (from Session 1.5; as needed for homework) • **Colored pencils or crayons**	
• **Materials from Session 2.6 except for M17**	
• **M12, Hundredths Grids or M21, Hundredths Grids for** *Fill Two* (from Sessions 1.3, 2.1; optional for Intervention) • **M17, Thousandths Grids** (from Session 1.5; optional for Intervention)	• **M27–M28, End-of-Unit Assessment** Make copies. (1 per student)

Overhead Transparency

Fill Two

Math Focus Points

◆ Representing decimal fractions as parts of an area

◆ Estimating sums of decimal numbers

◆ Using representations to add tenths, hundredths, and thousandths

Today's Plan			Materials
ACTIVITY **1 Introducing** *Fill Two*	15 MIN	CLASS	• M11; M21*; T68 ; M23*
ACTIVITY **2** *Fill Two*	35 MIN	PAIRS	• M11; M13; M21; M23 • Colored pencils or crayons
DISCUSSION **3 Adding Decimals**	10 MIN	CLASS	• M21
SESSION FOLLOW-UP **4 Daily Practice and Homework**			• *Student Activity Book*, pp. 43–44 • *Student Math Handbook*, pp. 63–65

*See *Materials to Prepare,* p. 83.

Ten-Minute Math

Practicing Place Value Say "five tenths," and ask students to write the number. Make sure that all students can read, write, and say this number correctly. Ask students to solve these problems mentally, if possible:

• What is $0.5 + 0.1$? $0.5 + 0.3$? $0.5 + 0.5$?

Have students compare each sum with 0.5. Ask students:

• Which places have the same digits?

• Which do not? Why?

If time remains, pose additional similar problems with the numbers 0.25 and 0.6.

① ACTIVITY
Introducing *Fill Two*

15 MIN   CLASS

Students begin their study of addition of decimals by using the Hundredths Grids for *Fill Two* (M21) and Decimal Cards Set A (M11) in the game *Fill Two*. Students played this game in Grade 4 in Unit 6, *Fraction Cards and Decimal Squares,* and may remember it.

Introduce the game by playing a round with the class playing against you, using the transparency of Hundredths Grids for *Fill Two* (T68). Students can refer to the copies of *Fill Two* (M23) as you play the game with students.

As you play the sample game with your class, ask questions that help students focus on looking at all four available Decimal Cards and thinking about the possibilities for filling up two of their Hundredths Grids. For the sample game discussed here, the teacher and class have already played two cards each. The teacher has played 0.7 and 0.35, respectively, on the top two grids, and the class has played 0.5 and 0.9, respectively, on the bottom two grids. These are the four Decimal Cards that are now facing up:

0.55 fifty-five hundredths	0.4 four tenths	0.85 eighty-five hundredths	0.3 three tenths

The goal of this game is to fill two of our grids as completely as we can. The important rule to remember is that we can't split up the decimal—we have to use the entire decimal on one grid. Look at the cards. Which card do you think I should play? Is there any card I can't play? Why not?

Give students a moment to discuss this with a partner. Establish that the 0.85 card cannot be played because there is not enough room on either grid. Gather a few suggestions.

I'm going to take Zachary's advice and use the 3 tenths card.

Using a different color than that used for 0.7, color in 0.3 on the first grid. Also write 0.7 + 0.3 below the grids. Draw another card and place it next to the other three.

Look at the cards again. Which card do you want to play? . . . Are there any cards you can't use? . . . Which card will get you closest to filling in one of the grids?

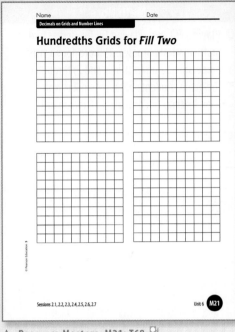

▲ **Resource Masters, M21; T68**

▲ **Resource Masters, M23**

Math Note

❶ **Playing *Fill Two*** Playing *Fill Two* serves two mathematical purposes: 1) It provides a visual model for adding fractions, and 2) through playing the game, students become familiar with combinations of decimals that add up to 1.

Play a few more cards to help students understand the rules of the game. The game ends when neither player can play one of the four face-up cards. (If only one player cannot play a card, that player loses that turn.) When the game ends, players write equations to show the amount colored on each grid and then the amount colored on both grids to see which player is closer to two. In the sample game, these were the cards played:

Teacher: 0.7 + 0.3   0.35 + 0.3 + 0.25

Class: 0.5 + 0.4   0.9 + 0.1

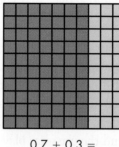
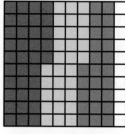

0.7 + 0.3 =   0.35 + 0.3 + 0.25 =

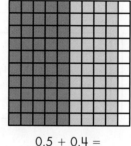

0.5 + 0.4 =   0.9 + 0.1 =

Ask about one of the easier sums or grids that have been completely filled in first. Then have students work on the other sums with a partner.

Let's figure out how much of each grid is colored in, and then the sum of how much is colored in on both grids. Who can tell me what 0.7 + 0.3 is? (one) *Who can tell me what 0.9 + 0.1 is?* (one) *Those were easy because they were only tenths, and the whole grid was filled in! Figure out what the other two sums are, and what the sum of both grids is. Who won the game?*

Ask students to explain how they determined the sum for each player. Remind students to refer to the grids to think about equivalents that will help them add (for example, to add 0.35 + 0.3 + 0.25, students may think of 3 tenths as 30 hundredths). Students may also recognize that the sum must be 0.9 because one tenth is left unshaded.❶

ACTIVITY
Fill Two

35 MIN   PAIRS

Students play *Fill Two* in pairs. As you circulate to help students learn how to play the game, notice how students are figuring out the sums of the decimals and whether they are paying attention to the place value of the digits in each number as they add.

ONGOING ASSESSMENT: Observing Students at Work

Using hundredths grids, students combine decimals.

- **How do students determine how much of a grid to color to match a chosen card?** Do they shade in decimal amounts correctly?

- **How do students choose cards to play?** Do they examine their partially colored-in grids to choose a card that will fill the grid? Are they able to figure out how much of the grid is not yet colored in? Do they pay attention to their opponent's grids?

- **How do students combine the decimals to show the total?** Do they use the representation? If so, do they have an efficient way to figure out how many squares are shaded? Do they use the part not yet shaded in and subtract that from one? Do they use the place value of the digits in the numbers as they add (i.e., adding tenths to tenths and hundredths to hundredths)? Do they use equivalents that they know?

DIFFERENTIATION: Supporting the Range of Learners

Intervention Some students will depend heavily on the grids to find the sum of the decimals. If students are counting filled squares on the grids, encourage them to count in efficient ways, for example, by 10s or 20s, to find the sum. Also encourage them to use the number of unfilled squares to determine the sum (e.g., if five squares or 0.05 is unfilled, how much of the grid is filled?).

Extension Students who easily play the game with Decimal Cards, Set A (M11) can include Decimal Cards, Set B (M13) in their deck. As these students begin playing with decimals in the thousandths, check to see whether they know how to color in thousandths on the hundredths grid (e.g., to shade in 0.125, they shade in $12\frac{1}{2}$ squares). Can students explain to you how they know that 5 thousandths is represented by a half square on the hundredths grid? These students can also play the variation, *Fill Four,* described at the bottom of the directions for the game.

Math Note

❷ **Showing Addition of Decimals on Grids** Using the grids for addition of decimals provides a visual model for students. By shading in the decimals, students keep track of the meaning of the numbers, that 0.3 is three tenths, and that 0.45 is 45 hundredths, or four tenths and five hundredths. When students manipulate numbers without retaining their sense of the meaning of those numbers, they may add decimals as if they are whole numbers (e.g., they add 0.3 + 0.45 and get an incorrect sum of 0.48). As the Investigation continues, remind students to actually shade in or to visualize decimal fractions on the hundredths grids. Some students will continue to use the grids throughout this Investigation. Other students, who have developed a mental model of the meaning of these numbers, will be able to add the decimals without using the grids. All students should be encouraged to think about the meaning of the numbers and their relationship to landmarks—are the decimals they are adding close to zero, $\frac{1}{2}$, or one? Does their answer make sense?

DISCUSSION

3 Adding Decimals

10 MIN   CLASS

Math Focus Points for Discussion

◆ Estimating sums of decimal numbers

◆ Using representations to add tenths, hundredths, and thousandths

Make sure that copies of Hundredths Grids for *Fill Two* (M21) are available during this discussion.❷ Write this equation on the board and ask students for an estimate of the sum:

$$0.3 + 0.45 + 0.15 =$$

Without solving this exactly yet, what would be a good estimate for the sum? Is it close to $\frac{1}{2}$, close to one, or more than one?

After gathering a few ideas about an estimate, ask students to solve the problem, and then compare answers with a partner.

Ask for volunteers to explain how they solved this problem. As students explain their strategies, ask other students to comment on them and to compare their own strategies.

Does anyone have questions for Stuart? Who else did it this way?

Possible strategies include the following:

- Shading in the decimals on a hundredths grid, noticing that one column or 0.1 is left unshaded, and concluding that the shaded area is 0.9, because $0.9 + 0.1 = 1$

- Shading in the decimals and recognizing that nine columns shaded represents 0.9

- Adding the decimals using decimal equivalents and known combinations of whole numbers

- Adding the decimals by place

Students might say:

"I added the 45 hundredths and the 15 hundredths, that was 60 hundredths. It's just like adding 45 and 15, only they're hundredths. I know that three tenths is the same as 30 hundredths, so it's 90 hundredths, or 9 tenths."

"I pictured the hundredths grid in my head. First I just thought about the tenths in each number and added three, four, and one and that's eight columns filled in. Five hundredths and five hundredths fills up another column, or another tenth, so the answer is 9 tenths."

Use students' explanations to focus attention on the place values of the digits in the numbers.

I noticed that when Lourdes added 0.60 and 0.3 she got 0.9 or 0.90. What do you notice about how Lourdes considered the place value of the decimals? . . . Why isn't the answer 0.63?

Benito really paid attention to the place value of the decimals, adding three tenths, four tenths, and one tenth. He also pictured what that would look like on a hundredths grid, and that seemed to help him.

Let students know they will be spending the rest of the Investigation studying and practicing the addition of decimals.

SESSION FOLLOW-UP

4 Daily Practice and Homework

 Daily Practice: For ongoing review, have students complete *Student Activity Book* page 43.

 Homework: Students use monthly precipitation averages to practice ordering decimals on *Student Activity Book* page 44.

 Student Math Handbook: Students and families may use *Student Math Handbook* pages 63–65 for reference and review. See pages 147–151 in the back of this unit.

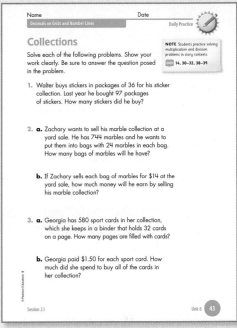

▲ **Student Activity Book, p. 43**

▲ **Student Activity Book, p. 44**

The Jeweler's Gold

Math Focus Points

◆ Estimating sums of decimal numbers

◆ Using representations to add tenths, hundredths, and thousandths

◆ Adding decimals to the thousandths through reasoning about place value, equivalents, and representations

Vocabulary

place value

Today's Plan		Materials
① ACTIVITY **Jeweler's Gold**	🕐 40 MIN 👥 GROUPS	• *Student Activity Book,* p. 45 • M11; M13; M12 or M21; M17; M23 • Markers; construction paper or chart paper
② DISCUSSION **Explaining Solutions**	🕐 20 MIN 👥 CLASS	• Jeweler's Gold posters (completed in the activity)
③ SESSION FOLLOW-UP **Daily Practice and Homework**		• *Student Activity Book,* pp. 46–47 • *Student Math Handbook,* pp. 63–65

Ten-Minute Math

Practicing Place Value Say "sixty-five hundredths," and ask students to write the number. Make sure that all students can read, write, and say this number correctly.

Ask students to solve these problems mentally, if possible:

• What is $0.65 + 0.3$? $0.65 + 0.4$? $0.65 + 0.05$?

Have students compare each sum with 0.65. Ask students:

• Which places have the same digits?

• Which do not? Why?

If time remains, pose additional similar problems with the numbers 0.15 and 0.75.

ACTIVITY

1 Jeweler's Gold

40 MIN GROUPS

Read the following numbers aloud and ask students to write them down. They can check with a partner or as a whole class to make sure that they have written the numbers down correctly. (Students may or may not use the zero in the ones place; either .3 or 0.3 is correct.)❶

0.3   1.14   0.085

Ask students to name the places for each digit in 0.085 (tenths, hundredths, thousandths). Also ask them about the relationship of each number to landmarks: are they closer to 0, $\frac{1}{2}$, 1, $1\frac{1}{2}$, or 2?

For this activity, each group of three solves the problem on *Student Activity Book* page 45 and makes a poster to show their reasoning.

Ask students to read through the directions. If needed, have one student read the directions to the whole class and ask a couple of students to restate the directions in their own words.

Students have about 40 minutes to solve the problem and make their posters, making sure that they explain their solution clearly. If they have additional time or do not all agree on the same answer, they should solve the problem by using a different strategy to check their first one.

As students finish their posters, they should put them up in the room. As more work is posted, students should look at one another's work. You can assign each group to look particularly carefully at one other group's poster and to jot down comments and questions.❷

In Jeweler's Gold, *students add decimals in real-life contexts.*

Teaching Notes

❶ **The Jeweler's Problem** This problem was created by a field-test teacher and is adapted from a case written by that teacher. (See Schifter, Deborah, Bastable, Virginia, & Russell, Susan Jo. *Developing Mathematical Ideas.* Number and Operations, Part 1: Building a System of Tens. Parsippany, NJ: Dale Seymour Publications, 1998, pages 114-120.)

❷ **Thinking Through the Jeweler's Problem**
Although students have not yet worked on a problem like this that involves adding tenths, hundredths, *and* thousandths, they have been working on the meanings of these numbers throughout the unit. By thinking through this problem for themselves, without a model for solving it, they use what they know about the meaning of the numbers and their experience with addition to develop a strategy. Experiences like these help students rely on their own resources to solve unfamiliar problems and, in the process, they deepen their understanding of mathematical relationships. Students' work in Grade 5 emphasizes the *meaning* of decimal fractions; the work on addition gives students a context in which to use and strengthen their understanding of that meaning. They will do much more work on computation with decimals in the middle grades.

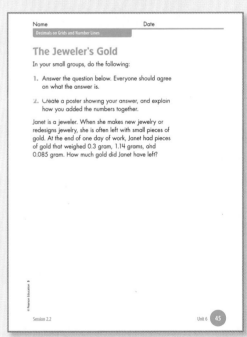

▲ **Student Activity Book, p. 45**

ONGOING ASSESSMENT: Observing Students at Work

Students add decimal fractions and explain their strategies.

- **Are students making sense of the meaning of the decimals?**
Do they realize that the sum should be about $1\frac{1}{2}$?

- **Are students paying attention to the decimal point and to the place value of each digit when they add?** For example, do they know that $1.14 + 0.3 = 1.44$, or that $0.3 + 0.085 = 0.385$? Do some students treat the numbers as if they were whole numbers, ignoring the place value of the digits (e.g., adding 1.14 and 0.3 and getting 1.17)?

- **What strategies are students using to add the numbers?** Do they use the hundredths grids? Do they use strategies they used for adding whole numbers, such as adding by place or adding on numbers in parts?

As you observe and interact with students, notice how they are solving the problem and ask questions to help them clarify and articulate what they understand about the meaning of the numbers.

- Read this decimal for me [0.3, 1.14, or 0.085]. What familiar numbers is this number close to? What would you expect the sum to be? Why do you think that is a reasonable sum?

- What is the meaning of 0.085? If you shaded it in on a thousandths grid, what would it look like? What if you shaded it in on a hundredths grid? Is it more or less than 0.3? How do you know?

- How did you add the decimals? Make sure you explain your method carefully on your posters. If [the principal, the teacher next door, the music teacher, etc.] walked in, would that person be able to understand clearly what problem you were solving and how you solved it from your poster?

DIFFERENTIATION: Supporting the Range of Learners

ELL English Language Learners may need some extra support in order to explain their reasoning. You can help by making one-on-one observations about their solutions as they work on their posters. Benito, I see that you added 0.3 and 0.085. Why was this your first step? (Because . . .) What was your next step? Repeat or rephrase students' explanations to help them articulate their ideas more clearly. If necessary, you can transcribe students' beginning ideas for them and have them copy your transcriptions onto their posters

Extension If some students finish quickly, check their posters and ask them to add to or revise their explanations if they are not clear or complete. Students can then play *Fill Two* while others finish their posters.

If some students are ready for an additional challenge, you can pose the following problem for them to solve in the same context of grams of gold:

$$2.05 + 0.76 + 1.3$$

DISCUSSION
Explaining Solutions

20 MIN   CLASS

Math Focus Points for Discussion

◆ Estimating sums of decimal numbers

◆ Adding decimals to the thousandths through reasoning about place value, equivalents, and representations

When most groups have put up their posters, bring the class back together and spend some time sharing students' approaches. It is not uncommon for students to make errors in this problem, particularly when adding 0.085 to the other numbers. If this is the case, acknowledge that this is a difficult problem and that they will be spending more time on addition of decimals. Use this discussion to compare the answers and to support students in thinking about the place value of the digits and estimating a reasonable result. Usually, by the time posters are shared, students have a good idea what the correct sum is, but it is useful for students to share mistakes they made along the way, especially those that involve treating a digit in one place as if it is in a different place.❸

It looks like we have some different strategies and some different answers. We know what the answer should be. Which group would like to explain its thinking and tell us either how you arrived at the correct answer, or, if you made a mistake, where your mistake was?❹

As groups share their thinking, ask who has questions for them, who agrees or disagrees, and why. Help students focus on the meaning of the numbers, their relationship to landmarks, and equivalents that they know—that 1.14 is a little more than one, that 0.3 is equivalent to $\frac{3}{10}$ and is less than $\frac{1}{2}$, that 0.085 is smaller than $\frac{1}{10}$, and that the sum should be about $1\frac{1}{2}$.

Summarize the strategies students in the class are using.

Math Note

❸ **Adding Decimals and Place Value** The key idea that should emerge from this discussion is that considering the place value of the digits is critical when adding decimal fractions or numbers with decimal portions, just as it is critical when adding whole numbers. The sum of 0.085 and 0.3 is not 0.088 any more than 880 is the sum of 85 and 30. Reminding students of what they know about adding whole numbers can be helpful here. The decimal point is a reference point that makes it clear which digits are in which places—ones, tens, hundreds, and so on from the decimal point moving to the left and tenths, hundredths, thousandths, and so on from the decimal point moving to the right.

Professional Development

❹ **Dialogue Box:** Adding Decimals: The Jeweler's Gold, p. 142

❺ **Teacher Note:** Adding Decimals, p. 132

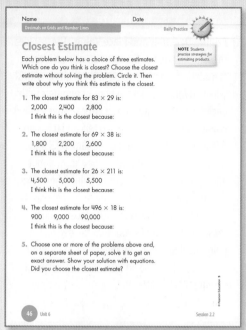

▲ **Student Activity Book, p. 46**

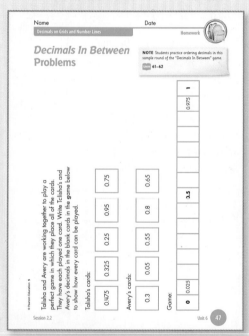

▲ **Student Activity Book, p. 47**

It looks like you're using a few different strategies to add decimals. Some of you are adding by place, adding the tenths, then the hundredths, and then the thousandths—just as you would do with whole numbers. Some of you started with one of the numbers, like Shandra's group which started with 1.14 and then added on the other numbers. Some of you shaded them on the hundredths and thousandths grids and then figured out what the whole amount was from putting those parts together on the grids. We're going to keep working on adding decimals, and talking about what strategies seem to work best.**⑤**

SESSION FOLLOW-UP

③ Daily Practice and Homework

 Daily Practice: For ongoing review, have students complete *Student Activity Book* page 46.

Homework: Students complete a sample round of *Decimals In Between* on *Student Activity Book* page 47.

 Student Math Handbook: Students and families may use *Student Math Handbook* pages 63–65 for reference and review. See pages 147–151 in the back of this unit.

Strategies for Adding Decimals

Math Focus Points

◆ Estimating sums of decimal numbers

◆ Using representations to add tenths, hundredths, and thousandths

◆ Adding decimals to the thousandths through reasoning about place value, equivalents, and representations

Today's Plan		Materials
ACTIVITY ① **Adding Decimals**	45 MIN CLASS INDIVIDUALS	• *Student Activity Book,* pp. 49–50 • M11; M13; M12 or M21; M17
DISCUSSION ② **Strategies for Adding Decimals**	15 MIN CLASS	• T68 (optional)
SESSION FOLLOW-UP ③ **Daily Practice**		• *Student Activity Book,* p. 51 • *Student Math Handbook,* pp. 63–65

Ten-Minute Math

Practicing Place Value Write 0.25 on the board and have students practice saying it. Let students know that this number is read as both "twenty-five hundredths" and as "point two five." Ask students:

• What is one tenth more than 0.25? What is 0.01 more? What is 0.05 less?"

Ask students how to write the new number and record it on the board. Then have them compare each sum or difference with 0.25. Ask students:

• Which places have the same digits?

• Which do not? Why?

If additional time remains, make up similar problems with the numbers 0.123 and 0.85.

Math Note

❶ **Contexts for Adding Decimals** As with the other operations and whole numbers, it is important for students to be able to create contexts to use when adding decimals. In this unit, several contexts are used—time, weight, and precipitation amounts. Help students develop other contexts that will make sense to them. Money is often used as a context for decimals, but it only works for tenths and hundredths, and sometimes students have a hard time thinking of 10 cents as one *tenth* because they think of this amount as either ten things (pennies) or one thing (a dime) rather than as a part of something.

ACTIVITY
1 Adding Decimals

45 MIN   CLASS   INDIVIDUALS

Show students these five Decimal Cards or write the decimals on the board:

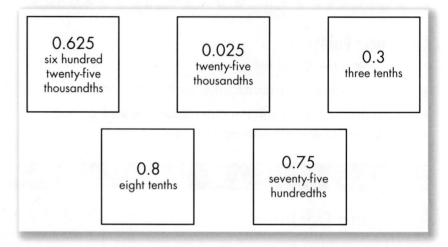

Look at these five decimals. Which three are the greatest? *(0.625, 0.8, 0.75)* How do you know? With a partner, I want you to think of a story problem for adding these three decimals.

Give students a few minutes to come up with a story context and collect a few examples.❶

Those are interesting contexts! Let's estimate what the sum to this addition problem will be. If you add $0.625 + 0.8 + 0.75$, is your answer going to be more than one? *(yes)* How do you know? Is the sum going to be more than $1\frac{1}{2}$? *(yes)* How do you know? More than two? *(yes, although students may not be as certain of this)* How do you know? We'll actually solve this problem later.

Today, you're going to be adding decimals by using the decimal cards, as we just did. You'll pick five, determine which three are the greatest, and add them. Think about contexts you can use to help you make sense of the problem. Make an estimate first so that you can tell whether your sum is reasonable, and think about our discussion in the last session of strategies for adding.

Students complete *Student Activity Book* pages 49–50.

Students practice adding decimals to the thousandths.

ONGOING ASSESSMENT: Observing Students at Work

Students add tenths, hundredths, and thousandths.

- **Are students paying attention to the decimal point and to the place value of each digit when they add?** Do some students treat the numbers as if they were whole numbers, ignoring the place value of the digits (e.g., if adding 0.8 and 0.75, do they get the right answer of 1.55 or do they get 0.83)?

- **What strategies are students using to add the numbers?** Do they use the hundredths grids? Do they use strategies they used for adding whole numbers, such as adding by place or adding on numbers in parts?

As students work, help them focus on the reasonableness of their answers and clarify and articulate their addition strategies by asking questions such as these:

- Read this decimal for me. What familiar numbers is this number close to? About what would you expect the sum to be? Why do you think that is a reasonable sum?

Name _____ Date _____

Decimals on Grids and Number Lines

Adding Decimals (page 1 of 2)

For each problem below, deal out five Decimal Cards and write them on the lines. Determine which three of the decimals have the greatest value, and add them. Show your work clearly.

1. Decimals: _____ _____ _____ _____ _____

   Addition problem: _____ + _____ + _____ = _____

2. Decimals: _____ _____ _____ _____ _____

   Addition problem: _____ + _____ + _____ = _____

3. Decimals: _____ _____ _____ _____ _____

   Addition problem: _____ + _____ + _____ = _____

Session 2.3   Unit 6   49

▲ **Student Activity Book, p. 49**

Name _____ Date _____

Decimals on Grids and Number Lines

Adding Decimals (page 2 of 2)

For each problem below, deal out five Decimal Cards and write them on the lines. Determine which three of the decimals have the greatest value, and add them. Show your work clearly.

4. Decimals: _____ _____ _____ _____ _____

   Addition problem: _____ + _____ + _____ = _____

5. Decimals: _____ _____ _____ _____ _____

   Addition problem: _____ + _____ + _____ = _____

6. Decimals: _____ _____ _____ _____ _____

   Addition problem: _____ + _____ + _____ = _____

50   Unit 6   Session 2.3

▲ **Student Activity Book, p. 50**

- What is the meaning of this number? If you shaded it in on a thousandths grid, what would it look like? What if you shaded it in on a hundredths grid?

- What strategy are you using to add decimals? Can you start with one number and add the others on in parts? Can you add all the tenths first, then the hundredths, and then the thousandths? How are you keeping track of what you've added?

DIFFERENTIATION: Supporting the Range of Learners

Intervention Students who are still having some difficulty interpreting numbers in the thousandths can begin by using only Set A of the Decimal Cards and adding only two cards. Encourage these students to use grids as needed. As they develop more confidence adding tenths and hundredths, they can add Set B to their cards, but still add only two cards.

ELL English Language Learners might need extra support during this activity. Let's think of a situation when we might add decimals together. If students get stuck, refer back to the grids they used to represent gardens in the previous Investigation. Let's say we have three gardens that are exactly the same size. One has 10 different *plots* for vegetables, another has 100, and the last one has 1,000. What is a story that could explain adding 0.625, 0.8, 0.75? Students should be able to create a context based on this scenario. In Lourdes's story, we want to know how much seed we need in order to plant corn in 0.8 of the first garden, 0.75 of the second, and 0.625 of the third garden. Let's add these values together to find our answer.

Extension Students who easily complete the task can add all five decimals, or they can choose the three least decimals to add.

DISCUSSION

2 Strategies for Adding Decimals

15 MIN   CLASS

Math Focus Points for Discussion

→ Estimating sums of decimal numbers

→ Adding decimals to the thousandths through reasoning about place value, equivalents, and representations

We're going to keep thinking about what strategies we use to add decimals. First, add these decimals that you thought about at the beginning of today's session. The story context you came up with may be helpful.

$$0.8 + 0.75 + 0.625$$

Give students a minute or two to solve this problem, and if they have time, check their work with a partner.

Ask a few students to explain their strategy for adding these numbers. You may want to have the transparency of Hundredths Grids for *Fill Two* (T68) for students to show the addition of these numbers on the grids.❷

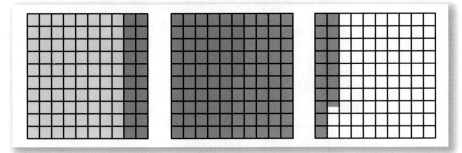

Does anyone have questions for Olivia? How did Olivia use place value or fractions, or decimal equivalents, or percents in adding decimals? Who else thinks they used the same strategy?

Who used a different strategy?❸

SESSION FOLLOW-UP

3 Daily Practice

Daily Practice: For ongoing review, have students complete *Student Activity Book* page 51.

Student Math Handbook: Students and families may use *Student Math Handbook* pages 63–65 for reference and review. See pages 147–151 in the back of this unit.

Professional Development

❷ **Dialogue Box:** Student Strategies for Adding Decimals, p. 145

❸ **Teacher Note:** Adding Decimals, p. 132

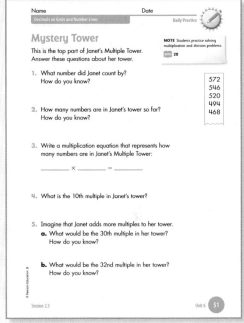

▲ **Student Activity Book, p. 51**

Decimal Problems

Math Focus Points

◆ Estimating sums of decimal numbers

◆ Using representations to add tenths, hundredths, and thousandths

◆ Adding decimals to the thousandths through reasoning about place value, equivalents, and representations

Today's Plan		Materials
① ACTIVITY **Decimal Problems**	🕐 30 MIN 👤 INDIVIDUALS	• *Student Activity Book,* pp. 52–53 • M12 or M21; M17
② DISCUSSION **Adjusting One Number**	🕐 15 MIN 👥 CLASS 👥 PAIRS	
③ ACTIVITY **Decimal Double Compare**	🕐 15 MIN 👥 CLASS 👥 PAIRS	• M11; M13; M22*
④ SESSION FOLLOW-UP **Daily Practice and Homework**		• *Student Activity Book,* pp. 54–55 • *Student Math Handbook,* pp. 63–65; G4

*See *Materials to Prepare,* p. 83.

Ten-Minute Math

Practicing Place Value Write 7.05 on the board and have students practice saying it. Let students know that this number is read as both "seven and five hundredths" and as "seven point zero five." Ask students:

• What is two tenths more than 7.05? What is 0.6 more? What is 0.08 more?"

Ask students how to write the new number and record it on the board. Then have them compare each sum with 7.05. Ask students:

• Which places have the same digits?

• Which do not? Why?

If additional time remains, make up similar problems with the numbers 5.45 and 20.3.

ACTIVITY

1 Decimal Problems

30 MIN INDIVIDUALS

Students solve decimal addition problems on *Student Activity Book* pages 52–53. Inform students that Problem 5 (0.98 + 0.05 + 1.06) will be discussed at the end of the session, and if they finish early, they should check their solution to that problem (and others) with a partner. ❶

ONGOING ASSESSMENT: Observing Students at Work

Students add tenths, hundredths, and thousandths.

- **Are students paying attention to the decimal point and to the place value of each digit when they add?** Do some students treat the numbers as if they were whole numbers, ignoring the place value of the digits (e.g., adding 1.29 and 3.654 in Problem 3 and getting 3.783)?

- **What strategies are students using?** Do they use the grids? Do they use strategies similar to those used for adding whole numbers, such as adding by place, or adding on numbers in parts?

- **For Problem 5, do any students think about adding one instead of 0.98 and then subtracting 0.02?**

As students work, help them focus on the reasonableness of their answers and help them clarify and articulate their addition strategies by asking questions such as these:

- Read this decimal for me. What familiar numbers is this number close to? About what would you expect the sum to be? Why do you think that is a reasonable sum?

- What is the meaning of this number? If you shaded it in on a thousandths grid, what would it look like? What if you shaded it in on a hundredths grid?

- What strategy are you using to add decimals? Can you start with one number and add the others on in parts? Can you add all the tenths first, then the hundredths, and then the thousandths? How are you keeping track of what you've added?

Look for the range of strategies your students are using to solve Problem 5 and ask some students to prepare to share their solutions. If some students try to add one instead of 0.98, and then compensate by subtracting, include this approach in those ready to be shared.

---

❶ **English Language Learners** It will be helpful to preview some of these problems with English Language Learners prior to this activity. Let's take the following decimals: 0.45, 0.09, and 1.01. What *familiar* numbers are these decimals close to? Remember, *familiar* numbers are numbers that you know, or recognize like 0, $\frac{1}{2}$ or 1. Encourage students to write and say each value out loud. Next, ask students to estimate a *reasonable sum* of these numbers. Explain what *reasonable sum* means. A *reasonable sum* makes sense based on the information we have. It should be *close to* the *exact* sum, but it may be a little more or a little less. What would be a *reasonable sum* for 0.45, 0.09, and 1.01?

Name _____ Date _____

Decimals on Grids and Number Lines

Decimal Problems (page 1 of 2)

Solve the problems below, showing your work clearly.

1. Shandra is preparing to run in a race. On Tuesday she ran 1.5 miles, on Thursday she ran 2.9 miles, and on Saturday she ran 2 miles. How many miles did she run altogether?

2. Mercedes finds two small pieces of gold in her jewelry tray. One weighs 0.48 gram and the other weighs 0.55 gram. How much gold did Mercedes find?

3. 1.29 + 3.654 = _____

4. Joshua is preparing for a race. On Monday he ran 1.75 miles, and on Wednesday he ran 1.6 miles. How many total miles did he run?

5. 0.98 + 0.05 + 1.06 = _____

52 Unit 6   Session 2.4

▲ **Student Activity Book, p. 52**

Math Note

② Changing One Number Many students use the strategy of changing one or more numbers when solving addition problems with whole numbers. This strategy continues to be useful when adding decimals but requires a careful focus on how the value of the number is changed. Most students understand why it makes sense to change 0.98 to 1 to make the addition easier, but some students will be unsure about the number that was added to 0.98—is it 2 tenths or 2 hundredths? Using or visualizing a hundredths grid helps most students clarify what amount must be subtracted.

Name _____ Date _____

Decimals on Grids and Number Lines

Decimal Problems (page 2 of 2)

Find the total amount of precipitation for the 3 months in the tables below, showing your work clearly. All amounts are recorded in inches.*

6.

City	Jan.	Feb.	May	Total
Sacramento, California	3.73	2.87	0.27	

7.

City	Sept.	Oct.	Nov.	Total
Helena, Montana	1.15	0.6	0.48	

8.

City	Jan.	Feb.	March	Total
Lincoln, Nebraska	0.54	0.72	2.09	

9.

City	Jan.	Feb.	March	Total
Harrisburg, Pennsylvania	2.84	2.93	3.28	

10.

City	June	July	Sept.	Total
Austin, Texas	3.72	2.04	3.3	

*Data are monthly averages for the years 1961–1990.

Session 2.4   Unit 6 **53**

▲ **Student Activity Book, p. 53**

DIFFERENTIATION: Supporting the Range of Learners

Intervention Students who are using the grids to add may need help understanding how to use the grids to represent numbers greater than one. Initially they fill entire grids to represent whole numbers (e.g., if the number is 1.29, they color one whole grid and 29 hundredths of another). Encourage them to think about how to use the grids for only the decimal portion of the number while still keeping track of the whole-number portion.

15 MIN   CLASS   PAIRS

DISCUSSION

② Adjusting One Number

Math Focus Points for Discussion

◆ Adding decimals to the thousandths through reasoning about place value, equivalents and representations

Write Problem 5 from *Student Activity Book* page 52 on the board or overhead.

$$0.98 + 0.05 + 1.06 =$$

Ask for a few students to share their strategies. Record each approach and ask how many other students used similar strategies. Focus on the approach of adding 1 instead of 0.98; either refer to a student's solution or bring it up yourself.

I noticed that when Tamira solved this problem she first added these numbers: $1 + 0.05 + 1.06$. Why do you think she did that? [Or: What if I started this way? Why would I do that?] . . . What did she have to do to finish solving the problem? Talk to a neighbor and see whether you can figure out what she did, and what she should do next to get the correct sum for the original problem. Using a story context or other model may help you think about this.

Give students a minute or so to discuss this with a neighbor and then ask for students to explain their thinking. It is important for students to understand that Tamira added 0.02 to 0.98 to get 1, and so 0.02 must be subtracted from 2.11 to get the correct sum of 2.09.②

ACTIVITY

3 Decimal Double Compare

15 MIN   CLASS   PAIRS

Introduce *Decimal Double Compare* by playing a few rounds with the class. Students can refer to copies of *Decimal Double Compare* (M22) for directions. Use only Decimal Cards, Set A (M11).

We're going to learn a new game, although it probably will seem familiar. It's called Decimal Double Compare. *It's pretty simple. Each player turns over two Decimal Cards, and whoever has the larger sum wins, and gets to take all four cards.*

Write these cards on the board.

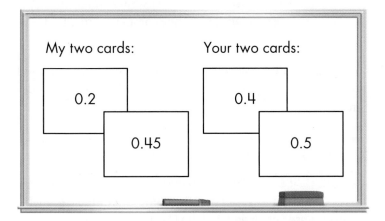

My two cards: Your two cards:

0.2
0.45

0.4
0.5

Look at these cards. Who would have the larger sum if we added the two cards together? Think about the relationship of the numbers. You may not even have to add to figure out which sum is greater.

Give students a minute or two to discuss this with a neighbor. Ask students to explain how they figured out which pair of cards has a larger sum.

Students might say:

"Those are really easy to add, I could just do it in my head. You have 65 hundredths, and we have 9 tenths, or 90 hundredths. We win!"

"I just compared the cards. Five tenths is bigger than 45 hundredths, and 4 tenths is bigger than 2 tenths, so our sum has to be bigger."

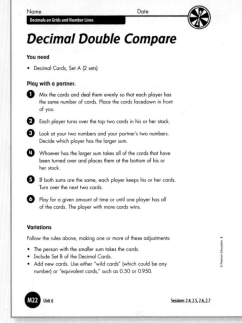

Name _____ Date _____

Decimals on Grids and Number Lines

Decimal Double Compare

You need
- Decimal Cards, Set A (2 sets)

Play with a partner.

❶ Mix the cards and deal them evenly so that each player has the same number of cards. Place the cards facedown in front of you.

❷ Each player turns over the top two cards in his or her stack.

❸ Look at your two numbers and your partner's two numbers. Decide which player has the larger sum.

❹ Whoever has the larger sum takes all of the cards that have been turned over and places them at the bottom of his or her stack.

❺ If both sums are the same, each player keeps his or her cards. Turn over the next two cards.

❻ Play for a given amount of time or until one player has all of the cards. The player with more cards wins.

Variations

Follow the rules above, making one or more of these adjustments:

- The person with the smaller sum takes the cards.
- Include Set B of the Decimal Cards.
- Add new cards. Use either "wild cards" (which could be any number) or "equivalent cards," such as 0.50 or 0.950.

M22 Unit 6   Sessions 2.4, 2.5, 2.6, 2.7

▲ **Resource Masters, M22**

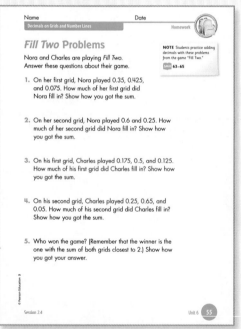

▲ **Student Activity Book, p. 54**

▲ **Student Activity Book, p. 55**

Some students estimate, for example, since 0.4 and 0.5 are either equal to or close to $\frac{1}{2}$, the sum is close to 1, and just by looking at the tenths of the other two cards (0.2 and 0.4), they see that the sum is just a little more than $\frac{1}{2}$.

For the remainder of the session, students play *Decimal Double Compare.*

ONGOING ASSESSMENT: Observing Students at Work

Students compare the sums of pairs of Decimal Cards.

- **How are students determining which pair of cards has the greater sum?** Are they adding every time? Do they add correctly?

- **Do students reason about the number relationships to determine who wins?** Do they compare cards? Do they use landmarks?

As you circulate to watch students play, ask students to read the numbers to you, and to explain how they decided which pair of cards has the greater sum.

DIFFERENTIATION: Supporting the Range of Learners

Extension Students who find it easy to compare the sums of two Decimal Cards can play the game with three Decimal Cards and/or use Sets A and B of the Decimal Cards.

SESSION FOLLOW-UP

Daily Practice and Homework

 Daily Practice: For reinforcement of this unit's content, have students complete *Student Activity Book* page 54.

 Homework: Students practice adding decimals with problems from *Fill Two* on *Student Activity Book* page 55.

Student Math Handbook: Students and families may use *Student Math Handbook* pages 63–65 and G4 for reference and review. See pages 147–151 in the back of this unit.

Decimal Games—Part 1

Math Focus Points

◆ Estimating sums of decimal numbers

◆ Adding decimals to the thousandths through reasoning about place value, equivalents, and representations

Today's Plan		Materials
1 ACTIVITY **Introducing** *Close to 1*	15 MIN · CLASS · PAIRS	• *Student Activity Book,* p. 57 • M11; M13; M24*; T69
2 MATH WORKSHOP **Adding Decimals** **2A** *Close to 1* **2B** *Decimal Double Compare* **2C** *Decimal Addition Problems* **2D** *Fill Two* (optional)	45 MIN	**2A** • *Student Activity Book,* p. 57 • M11; M13; M12 or M21; M24; M25* **2B** • *Student Activity Book,* p. 58 • M11; M22; M26* **2C** • *Student Activity Book,* pp. 59–61 **2D** • M11–M13; M21; M23 • Colored pencils or crayons
3 SESSION FOLLOW-UP **Daily Practice**		• *Student Activity Book,* p. 62 • *Student Math Handbook,* pp. 63–65; G1, G4

*See *Materials to Prepare,* p. 85.

Ten-Minute Math

Practicing Place Value Say "twenty-five thousandths," and ask students to write the number. Make sure that all students can read, write, and say this number correctly.

Ask students to solve these problems mentally, if possible. Ask students:

• What is $0.025 + 0.02$? $0.025 + 0.07$? $0.025 - 0.007$?

Have students compare each sum or difference with 0.025. Ask students:

• Which places have the same digits?

• Which do not? Why?

If time remains, pose additional similar problems with the numbers 1.15 and 2.5.

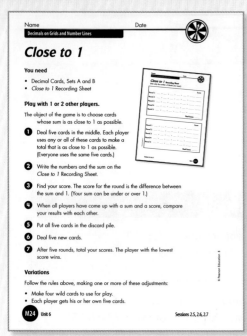

▲ Resource Masters, M24

ACTIVITY

1 Introducing *Close to 1*

15 MIN   CLASS   PAIRS

Introduce *Close to 1* by playing a few rounds with the whole class. Students can refer to copies of *Close to 1* (M24).

Deal out five cards and write the numbers on the board.

This sample introduction uses these five cards:

0.2 two tenths	**0.05** five hundredths	**0.45** forty-five hundredths

0.5 five tenths	**0.75** seventy-five hundredths

When you play this game, you deal out five cards and each player uses the same cards to get a sum as close to one as possible. Work with a partner to find a sum that's close to one. Just like the other "Close to" games we've played, your score is the difference between your sum and one. Your sum can be over or under one.

Give students a minute or two to solve the problem and find their score. If they finish quickly, encourage them to find other solutions to make sure that they are as close to one as possible. Ask students to share their solutions.

Students might say:

"We used 2 tenths and 75 hundredths. That's 95 hundredths so our score is 5 hundredths. . . . Oh wait! We could have used the 5 hundredths card and got 1!"

"We got 1, too! We used 45 hundredths, 5 tenths and 5 hundredths."

Model for students how to keep score on *Student Activity Book* page 57 by recording the first couple of rounds on the board, chart paper, or T69. If students seem to understand the rules of the game, they can start work on the Math Workshop. If some students seem uncertain, play another round or two with a small group to get them started.

MATH WORKSHOP

45 MIN

Adding Decimals

Students spend the rest of this session and most of the next two sessions in Math Workshop adding decimals by working on problems and playing the two games, *Decimal Double Compare* and *Close to 1.*

 **Close to 1**

PAIRS

See complete directions above and on *Close to 1* (M24). Students keep score on copies of *Close to 1* Recording Sheet (M25).

ONGOING ASSESSMENT: Observing Students at Work

Students add decimals to get a sum as close to one as possible.

- **What strategies are students using to get close to one?** Are they adding cards randomly? Are they using relationships they know to make combinations that total one (e.g., if one card is 0.45, they know that they need 0.55 to make one)?

- **How do students determine their score?** Are they able to find the score mentally? If not, what do they do?

DIFFERENTIATION: Supporting the Range of Learners

Intervention Students who are not yet comfortable working with thousandths should play with only Set A of the Decimal Cards, and may want to use the hundredths grids.

Name _____ Date _____

Decimals on Grids and Number Lines

Close to 1 Recording Sheet

(Use only the number of blanks you need.)

Score

Round 1: ___ + ___ + ___ + ___ + ___ = ___ ___
Round 2: ___ + ___ + ___ + ___ + ___ = ___ ___
Round 3: ___ + ___ + ___ + ___ + ___ = ___ ___
Round 4: ___ + ___ + ___ + ___ + ___ = ___ ___
Round 5: ___ + ___ + ___ + ___ + ___ = ___ ___

Final Score: _____

Score

Round 1: ___ + ___ + ___ + ___ + ___ = ___ ___
Round 2: ___ + ___ + ___ + ___ + ___ = ___ ___
Round 3: ___ + ___ + ___ + ___ + ___ = ___ ___
Round 4: ___ + ___ + ___ + ___ + ___ = ___ ___
Round 5: ___ + ___ + ___ + ___ + ___ = ___ ___

Final Score: _____

Sessions 2.5, 2.6, 2.7   Unit 6   57

▲ **Student Activity Book, p. 57;**
Resource Masters, M25; T69

Student Activity Book, p. 58

Name _____ Date _____

Decimals on Grids and Number Lines

Decimal Double Compare Recording Sheet

Choose five different rounds from *Decimal Double Compare* and record on this sheet. Use the <, >, or = signs between the cards. Write the sum of each pair below the cards.

1. Your cards: Partner's cards:

   ( )

   Sum: _____   Sum: _____

2. Your cards: Partner's cards:

   ( )

   Sum: _____   Sum: _____

3. Your cards: Partner's cards:

   ( )

   Sum: _____   Sum: _____

4. Your cards: Partner's cards:

   ( )

   Sum: _____   Sum: _____

5. Choose one round from above and explain how you determined which sum was greater.

58 Unit 6   Session 2.5

▲ **Student Activity Book, p. 58;**
Resource Masters, M26; T70

Name _____ Date _____

Decimals on Grids and Number Lines

Decimal Addition Problems (page 1 of 3)

Solve the problems below, showing your work clearly.

1. Nora takes three nuggets of gold to be weighed. One weighs 1.18 grams, another weighs 0.765 gram, and the third weighs 1.295 grams. What is the total weight of the gold?

2. On Monday Mercedes runs 2.25 miles, on Wednesday she runs 1.78 miles, and on Friday she runs 3.1 miles. How many total miles does she run?

3. On Tuesday Tavon runs 2.4 miles, on Thursday he runs 1.98 miles, and on Friday he runs 1.5 miles. How many total miles does he run?

4. Nora finds two more pieces of gold in her jewelry tray. One weighs 0.875 gram and the other one weighs 1.43 grams. What is the total weight of both pieces?

Sessions 2.5, 2.6, 2.7   Unit 6 59

▲ **Student Activity Book, p. 59**

PAIRS

2B Decimal Double Compare

Students can play *Decimal Double Compare* multiple times over the course of these two sessions. As they play, students fill in *Student Activity Book* page 58, *Decimal Double Compare* Recording Sheet, choosing a few of the rounds of the game to record. Use *Decimal Double Compare* Recording Sheet (M26) for extra copies of the recording sheet. Remind students to complete the recording sheet and to answer Question 5. If necessary, go over the directions on the recording sheet with students.

For a full description of this activity, see Session 2.4, pages 105–106.

INDIVIDUALS

2C Decimal Addition Problems

Students solve addition problems involving decimals on *Student Activity Book* pages 59–61. The discussion at the end of Session 2.6 focuses on Problem 1 on page 59.

ONGOING ASSESSMENT: Observing Students at Work

Students solve addition problems involving tenths, hundredths, and thousandths.

- **Can students make a reasonable estimate?**

- **Are students paying attention to the decimal point and to the place value of each digit when they add?** Do some students treat the numbers as if they were whole numbers, ignoring the place value of the digits?

- **What strategies are students using?** Do they use the grids? Do they use strategies similar to those used for adding whole numbers, such as adding by place, or adding on numbers in parts?

- **Can students use decimal equivalents; for example, representing all numbers in a problem as thousandths?**

- **Do students change a number to make an easier problem and then compensate for the change?** For example, in Problem 3, do they think of the problem as $2.4 + 2 + 1.5 - 0.02$?

As you watch students work, remind them to estimate a reasonable sum.

2D *Fill Two* (optional)

PAIRS

Students who are having a difficult time adding decimals in the thousandths will benefit from playing additional rounds of *Fill Two*. By coloring in the grids, students continue to develop their ideas about the value, and place value, of decimals in the thousandths, as well as their understanding of what it means to add decimals.

For a full description of this activity, see Session 2.1, pages 87–89.

SESSION FOLLOW-UP

3 Daily Practice

Daily Practice: For reinforcement of this unit's content, have students complete *Student Activity Book* page 62.

Student Math Handbook: Students and families may use *Student Math Handbook* pages 63–65 and G1, G4 for reference and review. See pages 147–151 in the back of this unit.

▲ Student Activity Book, p. 62

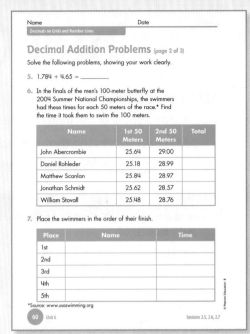

▲ Student Activity Book, p. 60

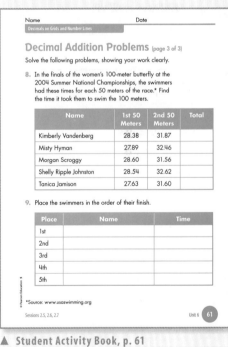

▲ Student Activity Book, p. 61

Decimal Games—Part 2

Math Focus Points

◆ Estimating sums of decimal numbers

◆ Adding decimals to the thousandths through reasoning about
place value, equivalents, and representations

Today's Plan		Materials
MATH WORKSHOP ❶ **Adding Decimals**	🕐 40 MIN	• *Student Activity Book*, pp. 57, 59–61 • M11–M13; M21–M26 • Colored pencils or crayons
DISCUSSION ❷ **Adding Decimals**	🕐 20 MIN 👥 CLASS	• *Student Activity Book*, p. 59 (begun in Session 2.5)
SESSION FOLLOW-UP ❸ **Daily Practice and Homework**		• *Student Activity Book*, pp. 63–64 • M12; M17 • *Student Math Handbook*, pp. 63–65; G1, G4

Ten-Minute Math

Practicing Place Value Say "three and nine hundred seventy-five thousandths," and
ask students to write the number. Make sure that all students can read, write, and say
this number correctly. Ask students to solve these problems mentally, if possible.

Ask students:

• What is $3.975 - 0.5$? $3.975 - 0.05$? $3.975 + 0.005$?

Have students compare each sum or difference with 3.975. Ask students:

• Which places have the same digits?

• Which do not? Why?

If time remains, pose additional similar problems with the numbers 5.075 and 6.35.

MATH WORKSHOP
Adding Decimals

40 MIN

For a description of the activities in this Math Workshop, see Session 2.5, pages 109–111.

DISCUSSION
Adding Decimals

20 MIN   CLASS

Math Focus Points for Discussion

◆ Estimating sums of decimal numbers

◆ Adding decimals to the thousandths through reasoning about place value, equivalents, and representations

Students share solutions to Problem 1 from *Student Activity Book* page 59.

Nora takes three nuggets of gold to be weighed. One weighs 1.18 grams, another weighs 0.765 gram, and the third weighs 1.295 grams. What is the total weight of the gold?

Ask students about their estimates for this problem.

How did you make an estimate for the sum? What whole number did you think the answer would be close to? Why?

Have several students write their solutions on the board or overhead and explain how they found the sum.

Students might say:

"I added the tenths, then the hundredths, then the thousandths. Then I added them together and added on the 2."

$$0.1 + 0.7 + 0.2 = 1$$
$$0.08 + 0.06 + 0.09 = 0.23$$
$$0.005 + 0.005 = 0.01$$
$$1 + 0.23 + 0.01 + 2 = 3.24$$

Sample Student Work

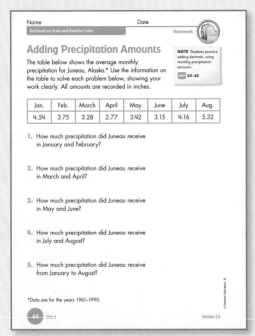

▲ Student Activity Book, p. 63

▲ Student Activity Book, p. 64

"I made all the numbers thousandths. Then I added them like they were whole numbers. I got 3,240 thousandths. So I know that every thousand thousandths is 1, so it's 3,240."

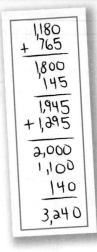

Sample Student Work

"I took one 'five'—that's five thousandths—from 0.765 and gave it 1.295, so that made it 0.76 and 1.3. I added 1.3 and 0.76. I could see the tenths made another one, so it was 2.06. Then I added on 1.18, so it was 3.24."

After each student explains, ask these questions:

Does anyone have questions for Deon? . . . What strategy did he use? How did he keep clear about which digits in the number represent tenths, hundredths, and thousandths? Who else used a strategy like this one? Who used a different strategy?

SESSION FOLLOW-UP
3 Daily Practice and Homework

 Daily Practice: For reinforcement of this unit's content, have students complete *Student Activity Book* page 63.

 Homework: Students use monthly precipitation averages to practice adding decimals on *Student Activity Book* page 64.

Student Math Handbook: Students and families may use *Student Math Handbook* pages 63–65 and G1, G4 for reference and review. See pages 147–151 in the back of this unit.

Decimal Games—Part 3

Math Focus Points

◆ Estimating sums of decimal numbers

◆ Adding decimals to the thousandths through reasoning about place value, equivalents, and representations

Today's Plan		Materials
① MATH WORKSHOP **Adding Decimals**	60 MIN	• *Student Activity Book,* pp. 57, 59–61 • M11–M13; M21–M26 • Colored pencils and crayons
② SESSION FOLLOW-UP **Daily Practice**		• *Student Activity Book,* p. 65 • *Student Math Handbook,* pp. 63–65; G1, G4

Ten-Minute Math

Practicing Place Value Write 0.008 on the board and have students practice saying it. Let students know that this number is read both as "eight thousandths" and as "point zero zero eight." Ask students:

• What is one tenth more than 0.008? What is 0.01 more? What is 0.003 more?

Ask students how to write the new number and record it on the board. Then have them compare each sum with 0.008. Ask students:

• Which places have the same digits?

• Which do not? Why?

If additional time remains, make up similar problems with the numbers 0.307 and 2.998.

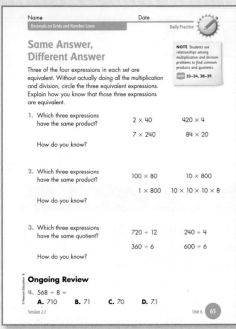

Name _____ Date _____

Decimals on Grids and Number Lines

Daily Practice

**Same Answer,
Different Answer**

NOTE Students use relationships among multiplication and division problems to find common products and quotients.

33–34, 38–39

Three of the four expressions in each set are equivalent. Without actually doing all the multiplication and division, circle the three equivalent expressions. Explain how you know that those three expressions are equivalent.

1. Which three expressions have the same product?

   2×40 420×4

   7×240 84×20

   How do you know?

2. Which three expressions have the same product?

   100×80 10×800

   1×800 $10 \times 10 \times 10 \times 8$

   How do you know?

3. Which three expressions have the same quotient?

   $720 \div 12$ $240 \div 4$

   $360 \div 6$ $600 \div 6$

   How do you know?

Ongoing Review

4. $568 \div 8 =$

   A. 710   **B.** 71   **C.** 70   **D.** 7.1

Session 2.7   Unit 6   65

▲ **Student Activity Book, p. 65**

MATH WORKSHOP

 Adding Decimals

60 MIN

For a description of the activities in this Math Workshop, see Session 2.5, pages 109–111.

If there is time, you can hold a discussion about one of the other problems on *Student Activity Book* pages 59–61 using the same format as the discussion in Session 2.6.

SESSION FOLLOW-UP

 Daily Practice

Daily Practice: For ongoing review, have students complete *Student Activity Book* page 65.

Student Math Handbook: Students and families may use *Student Math Handbook* pages 63–65 and G1, G4 for reference and review. See pages 147–151 in the back of this unit.

End-of-Unit Assessment

Math Focus Points

◆ Ordering decimals and justifying their order through reasoning about decimal representations, equivalents, and relationships

◆ Adding decimals to the thousandths through reasoning about place value, equivalents, and representations

Today's Plan		Materials
① **ASSESSMENT ACTIVITY** **End-of-Unit Assessment**	✓ 🕐 👤 60 MIN INDIVIDUALS	• M12 or M21 (optional); M17 (optional); M27–M28, End-of-Unit Assessment*
② **SESSION FOLLOW-UP** **Daily Practice**		• *Student Activity Book*, p. 66 • *Student Math Handbook*, pp. 61–62, 63–65

*See *Materials to Prepare,* p. 85.

Ten-Minute Math

Practicing Place Value Write 0.104 on the board and have students practice saying it. Let students know that this number is read both as "one hundred four thousandths" and as "point one zero four." Ask students:

• What is one tenth more than 0.104? What is 0.01 more? What is 0.09 more?

Ask students how to write the new number and record it on the board. Then have them compare each sum with 0.104. Ask students:

• Which places have the same digits?

• Which do not? Why?

If additional time remains, make up similar problems with the numbers 0.099 and 4.6.

Professional Development

① **Teacher Note:** End-of-Unit Assessment, p. 134

② **Assessment in This Unit,** p. 14

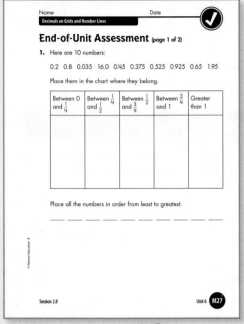

Name _____ Date _____

Decimals on Grids and Number Lines

End-of-Unit Assessment (page 1 of 2)

1. Here are 10 numbers:

   0.2 0.8 0.035 16.0 0.45 0.375 0.525 0.925 0.65 1.95

   Place them in the chart where they belong.

Between 0 and $\frac{1}{4}$	Between $\frac{1}{4}$ and $\frac{1}{2}$	Between $\frac{1}{2}$ and $\frac{3}{4}$	Between $\frac{3}{4}$ and 1	Greater than 1

   Place all the numbers in order from least to greatest.

   ___ ___ ___ ___ ___ ___ ___ ___ ___ ___

   Session 2.8   Unit 6 **M27**

▲ Resource Masters, M27

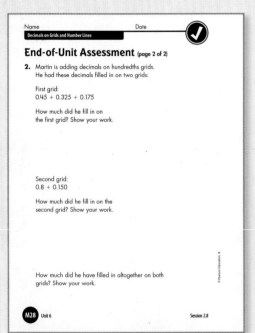

Name _____ Date _____

Decimals on Grids and Number Lines

End-of-Unit Assessment (page 2 of 2)

2. Martin is adding decimals on hundredths grids.
   He had these decimals filled in on two grids:

   First grid:
   0.45 + 0.325 + 0.175

   How much did he fill in on
   the first grid? Show your work.

   Second grid:
   0.8 + 0.150

   How much did he fill in on
   the second grid? Show your work.

   How much did he have filled in altogether on both
   grids? Show your work.

   M28 Unit 6   Session 2.8

▲ Resource Masters, M28

60 MIN INDIVIDUALS

① End-of-Unit Assessment

Students work individually on the End-of-Unit Assessment (M27–M28).
① ② This work focuses on two of the unit's benchmarks: Benchmarks 2 and 3.

In Problem 1, students order ten numbers that include whole numbers (e.g., 16.0), numbers with whole number and decimal fraction parts (e.g., 1.95), and decimal fractions that include tenths, hundredths, and/or thousandths (e.g., 0.02, 0.45, and 0.375). This problem addresses Benchmark 1: Order decimals to the thousandths.

In Problem 2, students add decimals to the thousandths in the context of the game *Fill Two*. This problem addresses Benchmark 3: Add decimal fractions through reasoning about place value, equivalents, and representations.

If time remains after students finish this assessment, they can play some of the decimal games from the unit and/or have a discussion about the assessment questions.

ONGOING ASSESSMENT: Observing Students at Work

Students solve two assessment problems. In the first, they classify 10 numbers between landmarks and then order them from smallest to greatest. In the second, they add decimal fractions in the context of *Fill Two*.

- **Do students place the numbers correctly, relative to the landmarks in the chart?**

- **Do students place the numbers in the correct order?**

- **In Problem 2, do students add the numbers correctly?**

- **Can students explain their solution in a way that shows that they understand the meaning of the numbers?** Do they base their methods on reasoning about a representation of decimals, using equivalents, or breaking up the numbers by place?

- **Do students notice whether their sums are reasonable?**

Remind students to explain their reasoning or show their method for all of the parts of Problem 2.

DIFFERENTIATION: Supporting the Range of Learners

Intervention If you can see that some students are having great difficulty ordering all of the numbers in Problem 1, modify the problem so that you get some information about what they understand. For example, ask them to choose five of the numbers that they feel confident about and order only those numbers. After they have done that, select one or two of the numbers that are left and ask students to try to place those numbers in the ordered list they have already made. In Problem 2, if some students are not adding the numbers successfully, especially in the first part of the problem, you may want to give them an additional problem so that you can assess more accurately what they do know. For example, can the student add tenths and hundredths but not thousandths? It would also be important to find out whether the student can accurately represent the numbers in the problem on a hundredths or thousandths grid.

Name _____ Date _____

Decimals on Grids and Number Lines   Daily Practice

Speed Skating

Here are some of the results from the 2006 Torino Winter Olympics Men's Short-Track Speed Skating Competition. Determine each competitor's rank in the men's 1,500-meter race.

NOTE Students solve real-world problems involving the math content of this unit.

58, 61–62

Rank	Country	Skater's Name	Time (in minutes: seconds)
	CAN	Charles Hamelin	2:26.375
	HUN	Peter Darazs	2:24.969
	KOR	Ho-Suk Lee	2:25.600
	ITA	Fabio Carta	2:24.658
	USA	Apolo Anton Ohno	2:24.789
	CHN	JiaJun Li	2:26.005
	KOR	Hyun-Soo Ahn	2:25.341
	CAN	Mathieu Turcotte	2:24.558
	NED	Niels Kersholt	2:24.962
	HUN	Viktor Knoch	2:26.806
	JPN	Satoru Terao	2:24.875

Explain your strategy for comparing the decimals.

66   Unit 6   Session 2.8

▲ **Student Activity Book, p. 66**

SESSION FOLLOW-UP

2 Daily Practice

  Daily Practice: For enrichment, have students complete *Student Activity Book* page 66.

  Student Math Handbook: Students and families may use *Student Math Handbook* pages 61–62, 63–65 for reference and renew. See pages 147–151 in the back of this unit.

Decimals on Grids and Number Lines

Teacher Notes

In Part 6 of *Implementing Investigations in Grade 5,* you will find a set of Teacher Notes that addresses topics and issues applicable to the curriculum as a whole rather than to specific curriculum units. They include the following:

Computational Fluency and Place Value

Computational Algorithms and Methods

Representations and Contexts for Mathematical Work

Foundations of Algebra in the Elementary Grades

Discussing Mathematical Ideas

Racial and Linguistic Diversity in the Classroom:
    What Does Equity Mean In Today's Math Classroom?

Dialogue Boxes

Teacher Note

About Teaching Decimals, Fractions, and Percents Together

Note: A similar Teacher Note is found in Unit 4. However, this version contains additional information about the ideas in this unit.

Fractions, percents, and decimals can all be used to show numbers less than one and numbers between whole numbers. In practice, each form has come to be used for certain purposes more than others. For example, we are more likely to use fractions for objects that we split up and for measurements used in daily life: $\frac{1}{4}$ cup of flour, $\frac{3}{4}$ of a yard of fabric, $\frac{1}{2}$ an hour, $\frac{1}{3}$ of the class. We use decimals as part of certain measurements: 25.3 miles on the car's odometer, 9.6 gallons of gas, 98.6 degrees, $3.25, 10.5 inches of rain. Percentages are often used for prices, costs, changes in rates, and parts of large groups: 25% off sale, a 3% salary increase, 10% unemployment, 40% of teenagers.

The fractions, decimals, and percents students study in Grade 5 are all rational numbers. Rational numbers are numbers that can be expressed as the division of two integers; that is, as a fraction with an integer in the numerator and in the denominator. The word *rational* refers to the fact that these numbers can all be expressed as a ratio of integers. The rational numbers include all the integers ($\ldots -3, -2, -1, 0, 1, 2, 3, \ldots$). Any of these numbers can be expressed as a fraction with a denominator of 1, such as $34 = \frac{34}{1}$, and $-100 = \frac{-100}{1}$, as well as in other forms; for example, 34 is also equivalent to $\frac{68}{2}$. Rational numbers also include fractions such as $\frac{1}{2}$ and $\frac{11}{12}$, mixed numbers such as $3\frac{1}{2}$ (which can be expressed as $\frac{7}{2}$), and decimals such as 0.05 and 0.125 (which can be expressed, respectively, as $\frac{5}{100}$ and $\frac{125}{1,000}$).

Learning about the different forms of rational numbers together helps students use knowledge of one form to understand the others. In this unit, students focus on equivalent fractions and decimals. Post the class "Equivalents" chart from Unit 4 and add to it during this unit.

Understanding decimals requires the coordination of images of quantities less than one that students have developed with decimal notation. Using what they know about fraction-decimal equivalents can help them understand what the digits to the right of the decimal point represent. Reading and writing notation for decimal fractions can be confusing because these numbers are named by the smallest place. For 0.3, we say "three tenths," but for 0.34, we say "thirty-four hundredths," and for 0.345 we say "three hundred forty-five thousandths." We do not say "3 tenths, 4 hundredths, and 5 thousandths" for 0.345, although that might make more sense to students just learning about these numbers! Using fraction equivalents helps students make sense of how $0.3 = \frac{3}{10} = \frac{30}{100} = \frac{300}{1,000}$, and, therefore, how 3 tenths, 4 hundredths, and 5 thousandths is equal to 345 thousandths. Facility with fraction equivalents helps students compare or compute with decimal fractions; for example, comparing 0.3 and 0.257 by thinking about their fraction equivalents, $\frac{300}{1,000}$ and $\frac{257}{1,000}$.

Students also draw on their knowledge of percents in their study of decimals. Percents and decimals are closely related because *percent* means "out of a hundred" or "hundredths": $75\% = \frac{75}{100} = 75 \times 0.01 = 0.75$. As students represent decimal fractions on hundredths and thousandths grids, they learn more about the fraction-percent equivalents they have worked with and their relationship to decimals. For example, they know that $\frac{1}{8} = 12\frac{1}{2}\%$. When they represent $\frac{1}{8}$ on hundredths and thousandths grids, they find that $\frac{1}{2}\%$ is equal to 5 thousandths: $\frac{1}{8} = 12\frac{1}{2}\% = \frac{12\frac{1}{2}}{100} = 0.125$.

A new focus in this unit is the interpretation of fractions as division. Students learn how an equivalent decimal fraction results from carrying out the division indicated by a fraction. Although students know, for example, that $\frac{1}{4} = 0.25$, they may think about this equivalence in the way they think of equivalent fractions: one out of four equal parts is equivalent to 25 out of 100 equal parts of the same quantity because four groups of 25 equals 100. They may visualize an area model, such as a 10×10 square that represents one, and divide it into four equal parts. They can then see that one of those parts is 25 out of 100 square units: one fourth of the square equals $\frac{25}{100}$. This model *is* one model of division: $1 \div 4 = \frac{1}{4}$ can be interpreted as "$\frac{1}{4}$ is one of the parts when 1 is divided into 4 equal parts," just as $8 \div 4 = 2$ can be interpreted as "two is one of the parts when eight is divided into four equal parts." Nevertheless, even though students have been modeling fractions as division, they may not be thinking explicitly that one meaning of a fraction as division. In this unit, this meaning is worked on explicitly. Students see that dividing 1 by 4 on the calculator results in 0.25, and then they think through the meaning of this division. Students spend several sessions finding decimal equivalents for fractions.

Studying fractions, percents, and decimals together helps students build their number sense about rational numbers. Knowledge of these relationships helps students estimate the result of calculations using any of these representations. It helps them carry out computation and catch computational errors because they use the equivalents they know to help them determine what a reasonable result to a problem should be. Finally, studying these ideas together gives students a better sense of how the different types of numbers are actually used in real life, as well as in particular mathematical contexts.

Teacher Note

Extending Place Value to Thousandths and Beyond

Students have spent a great deal of time in elementary school working with the place value of whole numbers. In Grade 4, they extended their knowledge of the base-ten system to tenths and hundredths. In this unit, students review their understanding of tenths and hundredths and focus on thousandths as well as on the place value of digits representing even smaller numbers.

The base-ten number system (also called the *decimal number system*) is a place-value system; that is, any numeral, such as 2, can represent different values, depending on where it appears in a written number: it can represent 2 ones, 2 tens, 2 hundreds, 2 thousands, and so forth. Understanding a place value system requires coordinating the way we write the numerals that represent a particular number (e.g., 5,217) and the way we name numbers in words (e.g., five thousand two hundred seventeen) with how those symbols represent quantities.

Numbers that include amounts less than one are represented as a continuation of the base-ten system with digits to the right of the decimal point. The decimal point separates the integer and fractional parts of the number. The structure of the place-value system continues to hold true for these digits to the right of the decimal point. A digit in any place represents a value ten times greater than the same digit in the place immediately to the right and one tenth of the value of the same digit in the place immediately to the left:

222.222

Two hundred twenty-two and two hundred twenty-two thousandths

From left to right, the digits represent 2 hundreds, 2 tens, 2 ones, 2 tenths, 2 hundredths, and 2 thousandths. The digit in the hundreds place represents a quantity ten times greater than the digit in the tens place. The digit in the hundredths place represents a quantity ten times greater than the digit in the thousandths place.

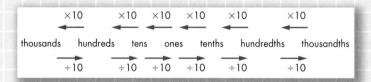

One of the problems for students in understanding decimals is that the amounts represented by tenths, and even more by hundredths and thousandths, are very small. They are much more experienced with whole numbers in their lives. Just as very large numbers are difficult to visualize, so are very small numbers. Students do not generally deal with hundredths and thousandths in their everyday experience or, when they do, it is difficult to actually perceive the magnitude of those numbers. For example, 0.1 second and 0.01 second both represent a very short amount of time—the difference between them is not perceptible without specialized tools. It is perhaps easier to distinguish between 0.1 mile and 0.01 mile, but these are not quantities that come up in students' everyday experience. Smaller amounts—0.001 second or mile—are even more difficult to imagine. Yet understanding that 0.1 is ten times bigger than 0.01 is crucial to understanding and computing with decimals. This same relationship holds true for whole numbers, such as 50 and 5 (50 is ten times bigger than 5, 5 is $\frac{1}{10}$ of 50), but both the change in magnitude and the actual size of the numbers are more obvious in real situations: there is a noticeable difference between 50 seconds and 5 seconds. Even though the structure of the place-value system is the same for digits that indicate the fractional part of the number, experience in classrooms is that students need time to develop an understanding of the quantity, order, and equivalence with regard to these very small numbers.

The decimal point is the conventional separator used in the United States to separate the integer part of a number from parts of the number that are less than 1. (See the Math Note in Session 1.3 about notation in other countries.)

One of the key understandings students should have developed in Grade 4 is that digits to the right of the decimal point indicate that the entire quantity is greater than the whole-number portion of the number and less than the next larger whole number (for positive numbers). For example, consider a swimmer who swims the 100-meter freestyle in 51.34 seconds. The part of the number represented by ".34" is a fractional amount: it took more than 51 seconds for the swimmer to complete the race, but less than 52 seconds.

Learning about numbers that include digits to the right of the decimal point is further complicated by the way we read the numbers. The decimal portion of 1.865 is conventionally read as "eight hundred sixty-five thousandths" rather than "8 tenths, 6 hundredths, and 5 thousandths." Students may at first read numbers in this second way, which actually indicates their understanding of the place value of each digit. Gradually students learn that 8 tenths, 6 hundredths, and 5 thousandths is equivalent to eight hundred sixty-five thousandths, which is the way the number is read. This number is also conventionally read as "one point eight six five," and students should also learn to recognize this as a common way of reading decimals.

The use of zeros in decimal notation can be confusing to students. Students should sometimes see decimal numbers that are less than one written with a zero in the ones place, such as 0.5. Including the zero helps remind students that the decimal point separates the whole number portion of the number (which, in this case, is zero) from the part that is less than one. However, students should also see numbers such as .5 written without the 0 in the ones place, so that they recognize that 0.5 = .5. The convention we have adopted for decimal notation in the *Investigations* units is to include a 0 in the ones place.

Students also learn about zeros in places to the right of nonzero digits, such as 0.5 = 0.50 = .500. Students are learning that 5 tenths (0.5), 50 hundredths (0.50), and 500 thousandths (0.500) are equal amounts. Recognizing these equivalencies is critical for comparing and computing with decimals. (Note that, mathematically, 0.5 and 0.50 are the same number; however, in statistics, science, and engineering, writing 0.5 or 0.50 may suggest a different level of confidence in the accuracy of results.)

In this unit, squares divided into tenths, hundredths, and thousandths are used as representations to help students visualize the relationship of these small numbers to one another and to 1. Students have been using representations similar to these to understand large numbers and fractions. Now, instead of building up 100, then 1,000, and then 10,000 from single square units they start with a single square unit and break it into smaller and smaller parts. What is critical is that students think of this square unit as one whole and the divisions of the square as equal parts of that one whole.

Teacher Note

Finding Decimal Equivalents of Fractions by Division

In this unit, students expand their understanding of decimal fractions (decimal representations for numbers that can be expressed as a division of two whole numbers, such as $\frac{25}{5}$, $\frac{1}{4}$, or $\frac{11}{10}$) by drawing on all of the work they have done with rational numbers in the form of fractions, percents, and decimals. In Grades 3 and 4 and in Grade 5 Unit 4, they developed a repertoire of fraction-percent equivalents and decimal equivalents for a few familiar fractions. In this unit, students should expand that repertoire as they increase their understanding of how digits to the right of the decimal point represent tenths, hundredths, thousandths, and beyond. Emphasis in this unit is on developing meaning for decimals to the thousandths. When students have a firm grasp of tenths, hundredths, and thousandths, they can easily expand their knowledge to places that represent even smaller numbers.

One part of the work on fraction-decimal equivalents in this unit will be new for most students—finding decimal equivalents of a fraction through division. Fractions are one way to represent division. Carrying out the indicated division results in a decimal representation of the number. For example, one way of interpreting $\frac{1}{4}$ is as $1 \div 4$. When you carry out this division on a calculator, the result is 0.25. When the non-zero denominator of a fraction is a factor of the numerator, as in $\frac{25}{5}$, the decimal equivalent is a whole number. In all other cases, there is at least one digit to the right of the decimal point.

In this unit, students reason about dividing the numerator by the denominator of some fractions to find their decimal equivalents and to use a calculator for other fractions. For example, students can reason about carrying out the division indicated by $\frac{1}{4}$. They can visualize this division and think of a context for it, as follows: "If I want to divide one garden into four equal plots, I can use the hundredths grid. There will be two columns of ten squares in each plot. Then I have two columns or twenty squares left. Each plot gets five more squares. That's 25 squares for each plot. It's 25 hundredths

or 0.25." This fraction-decimal equivalent is one that students already know from previous work, but thinking through how a fraction represents division in this way may be new.

As students work, help them articulate what they already know about the meaning of division. For example, one meaning of a division expression such as $6 \div 3$ or $\frac{6}{3}$ with which 5th graders are familiar is the size of one part when 6 is divided into three equal parts. Help them use this understanding to think through the meaning of a division expression such as $2 \div 3$ or $\frac{2}{3}$: the size of one part when 2 is divided into 3 equal parts. An alternative meaning of division—how many 3s are in 6?—may be one that students have used more often in the past, but whereas it is possible to use this meaning for division of a smaller by a greater number, such as $\frac{2}{3}$, it is often more difficult for fifth graders to use this interpretation.

There are several goals for the work students do dividing the numerator of a fraction by its denominator to find the decimal equivalent: 1) to make sense of how fractions can be interpreted as division; 2) to continue gaining familiarity with fraction-decimal equivalents that are frequently encountered (e.g., $\frac{1}{4} = 0.25$, $\frac{1}{8} = 0.125$); 3) to consider what a reasonable decimal equivalent is for less-familiar fractions (e.g., the decimal equivalent for $\frac{1}{11}$ must be less than 0.1); and 4) to be introduced to decimal equivalents for familiar fractions that cannot be represented exactly by a finite number of digits (e.g., the decimal representations for $\frac{1}{3}$ and $\frac{2}{3}$).

As your students use calculators to find decimal equivalents for fractions, they will notice that decimal equivalents for fractions fall into two main groups—decimals that terminate, or end after a certain number of digits, and decimals that fill the calculator display (nonterminating decimals). Most calculators found in elementary classrooms can accommodate eight digits. Because they usually display a 0 in the ones place for numbers less than one, they show a maximum of seven digits to the right of the decimal point.

Nonterminating decimal equivalents of fractions are called repeating decimals—some or all of the decimal digits repeat. The decimal equivalent for $\frac{5}{6}$ is 0.8333333 . . . . Only the 3 repeats. A repeating decimal with one repeating digit is notated as $0.8\overline{3}$. The decimal equivalent for $\frac{2}{22}$ is 0.1818181 . . . . This decimal can be notated as $0.\overline{18}$. For some fractions, such as $\frac{1}{3}$ ($0.\overline{3}$) or $\frac{1}{6}$ ($0.1\overline{6}$), the repeating pattern is obvious. For others, such as $\frac{1}{7}$ ($0.\overline{142857}$), it is not obvious from the digits on the calculator display.

Students do not yet have the mathematical tools and experience to be sure about the part of the decimal that repeats beyond the digits in the calculator display for many of the fractions they work with. They can think through the division of $\frac{1}{3}$ by using or visualizing tenths, hundredths, and thousandths grids: when thinking of dividing 1 into 3 equal parts, first divide up the tenths; 3 tenths are in each part, with one tenth left; the one tenth is equivalent to 10 hundredths; again 3 hundredths can be allocated to each part, with one hundredth left; the hundredth can be divided into 10 thousandths; 3 thousandths are in each of the three parts, with one thousandth left; and so on. Students can begin to see a pattern here—that this allocation of nine of the parts and splitting up of the remaining part into the next smallest power of ten will continue no matter how small the parts.

However, students are not expected to be able to think through and explain most of the repeating decimal patterns they encounter; this is just an introduction to the different kinds of decimals. You can let them know that they *have* found the repeating pattern; for example, that it is the first six digits of the decimal for $\frac{1}{7}$ that repeat. However, you should acknowledge that for some fractions there could be decimals that repeat beyond what they can see on the calculator display or that appear to have a complete repetition within the calculator display, but do not. For example, $\frac{47}{49}$ begins 0.9591836 and goes on for 42 decimal places before it repeats all 42 digits. For example, dividing 20,000,000 by 6,666,667 results in the terminating decimal 0.33333335. In a calculator display that shows only seven digits following the decimal point, this number would look like the repeating decimal $0.\overline{3}$ or $\frac{1}{3}$. However, although this division results in a number very close to $\frac{1}{3}$, it is not exactly $\frac{1}{3}$.

There are some numbers that *cannot* be expressed as the division of two integers. For example, the number π that is used in the formula for the area of a circle πr^2 is an infinite, nonrepeating decimal that can be only approximated by a fraction. It is not a rational number. Students will encounter such numbers later in their study of mathematics. They will also encounter other tools, such as the long division algorithm, that are useful for further investigating repeating and terminating decimals.

Assessment: Comparing and Ordering Decimals

Problem 1

Benchmarks addressed:

Benchmark 1: Read, write, and interpret decimal fractions to thousandths.

Benchmark 2: Order decimals to the thousandths.

In order to meet the benchmarks, students' work should show that they can:

• Place the five numbers in the correct order;

• Explain their reasoning, demonstrating an understanding of the values of the numbers.

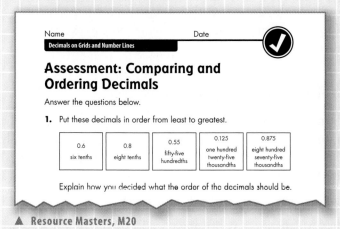

▲ Resource Masters, M20

Meeting the Benchmarks

Students who meet the benchmarks place the numbers in the correct order and give a clear explanation showing an understanding of the value of each number.

Deon orders the numbers correctly and explains that he thinks about these decimals in terms of their percent equivalents.

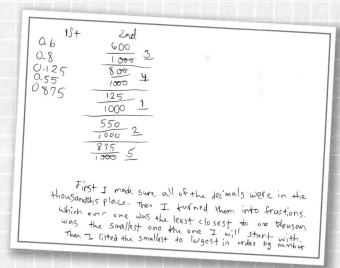

Deon's Work

Tamira also orders the numbers correctly. Her explanation includes finding the fraction equivalents in thousandths for each decimal, as well as considering that the smallest decimal is the one "least closest to one thousand," by which she seems to mean the fewest parts out of one thousand.

Tamira's Work

Avery considers the place value of the digits, recognizing that he can order three of the five numbers by the digit in the tenths place. He then uses the thousandths equivalent for 0.8 and compares 0.800 and 0.875. Avery's work shows an understanding of the value of each place and how to use that understanding to compare decimal fractions.

> I thought of all the numbers in the tenths and I put them in order like 0.1, 0.5, 0.6 and Since the last two where both 8 in the tenths, I pictured 0.8 in the thous + this + .875 was bigger than .800.

Avery's Work

Partially Meeting the Benchmarks

For this problem, most students either put all the numbers in the correct order or are unable to do so. Few students fit in this category of partially meeting the benchmarks. However, a few students may place the numbers in the correct order, but not offer a clear mathematical explanation.

For example, Benito places the numbers in the correct order but explains only how he decides that 0.125 is the smallest number. Benito visualizes how 0.125 can be represented as 125 out of 1,000 little squares.

> Smallest
> 0.125
> 0.55
> 0.6
> 0.8
> 0.875
> largest
>
> I know 0.125 is the smallest because it is only 125 out of 1,000 little squares

Benito's Work

Shandra also places the numbers in order correctly, but her explanation does not reveal any mathematical thinking, and thus it is unclear what she understands about the value of decimals.

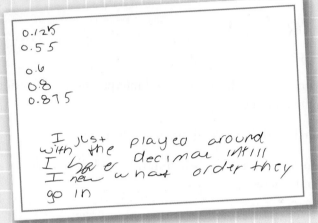

> 0.125
> 0.55
> 0.6
> 0.8
> 0.875
>
> I just played around with the decimal intill I knew what order they go in

Shandra's Work

It is likely that both of these students know more about ordering these numbers than they have written on paper. Interview them or ask them to write more to explain their reasoning.

Not Meeting the Benchmarks

Students who do not meet the benchmarks do not place the numbers in the correct order, and their explanations usually reveal that they do not understand the meaning and values of the decimals.

Cecilia has none of the numbers in the correct order, and her explanation is confusing. Cecilia should be asked what she means by the "other" number, which may help clarify her misconceptions or provide more insight into what she does and does not understand about interpreting decimal notation.

> 0.55, 0.125, 0.875, 0.6, 0.8
>
> I put the decimals in this order because I know that the farther away the other number is away from zero the less the number will be.

Cecilia's Work

Stuart's explanation is a valid explanation for ordering decimals (looking at the place value of each digit) but that explanation is not supported by his work. He did place the numbers in the correct order. It may be that he can interpret tenths and hundredths and compare thousandths to thousandths by simply comparing them as if they are whole numbers, but he may not be able to coordinate all three places.

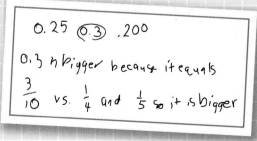

Stuart's Work

Cecilia and Stuart will both benefit from shading in these decimals on grids, as well as working on decimal equivalents, such as 0.8 = 0.80 = 0.800. For example, they can shade in 0.8 on a hundredths grid and a thousandths grid, and discuss how those representations are the same and how to represent them with fractions and decimals. These students can also benefit from ordering small sets of the Decimal Cards, perhaps five cards at a time, shading in grids to help them order the cards.

Problem 2

Benchmarks addressed:

Benchmark 1: Read, write, and interpret decimal fractions to thousandths.

Benchmark 2: Order decimals to the thousandths.

This question addresses the same benchmarks as Question 1 but also requires students to interpret 0.200. None of the numbers in the first problem included a zero to the right of the decimal point.

In order to meet the benchmarks, students' work should show that they can:

- Identify 0.3 as the greatest number;

- Explain their reasoning, demonstrating an understanding of the values of the numbers.

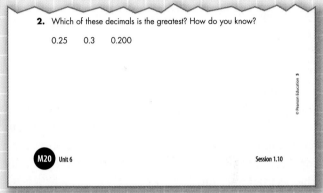

▲ **Resource Masters, M20**

Meeting the Benchmarks

Students who meet the benchmarks identify 0.3 as the largest decimal, and their explanation is mathematically clear.

Alicia uses fraction equivalents for each decimal, $0.25 = \frac{1}{4}$, $0.3 = \frac{3}{10}$, and $0.200 = \frac{1}{5}$. She correctly identifies 0.3 as being the greatest decimal. Alicia's explanation could be more complete; she does not explain how she knows that $\frac{3}{10}$ is greater than $\frac{1}{4}$ and $\frac{1}{5}$. However, it is clear that she understands the values of the decimal fractions. She could be asked to provide a more complete explanation.

Alicia's Work

Joshua uses the tenths place to compare the decimals and correctly identifies 0.3 as the greatest decimal.

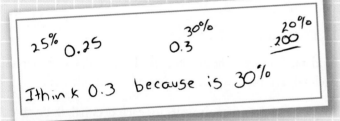

0.3 You only need to use the tenths place and $\frac{3}{10}$ is more than $\frac{2}{10}$.

Joshua's Work

Samantha uses percent equivalents, which are written next to each decimal to identify 0.3 as the greatest decimal because it is 30%. Although she does not explain in words why 30% is greater than 25% and 20%, percentages can be compared directly in the way that whole numbers are compared. Her work shows that she understands the values of the decimal fractions.

25% 0.25   30%
0.3   20%
                                   .200

I think 0.3 because is 30%

Samantha's Work

Partially Meeting the Benchmarks

As with Problem 1, students usually either solve this problem correctly with reasonable explanations or incorrectly. However, students who identify the answer but have weak or confusing explanations partially meet the benchmarks. It is important for students to learn how to provide good explanations of their mathematical thinking. It would be important practice for these students to discuss their thinking with you or with another student and then write a more complete justification for their answer to the problem.

Lourdes makes thousandths equivalents for each decimal (0.250, 0.300, 0.200), which is one method many students use to compare decimals. However, it is not clear what Lourdes means by "take away the zeroes." Because the rest of her reasoning is good—for example, she knows that "0.25 would be in the middle of 0.30 and 0.20," it would be important to ask her to explain what she means more fully. Is there some confusion in her interpretation of decimal notation or do her words not adequately express her thinking?

0.250   0.300   0.200

I think 0.300 is greater because if you take away true zeros, 0.200 would be the smallest and 0.25 would be in the middle of .30 and .20.

Lourdes's Work

Zachary identifies 0.3 as the greatest decimal and he also shows elements of good thinking, but his explanation does not show how he knows that 0.2 and 0.25 are less than 0.3. It may be that these relationships seem so evident to him that he does not realize that he needs to provide further justification. If that is the case, helping him to imagine an audience that needs explanation can be helpful. "What if you were explaining this to a third grader who didn't understand what these numbers mean?"

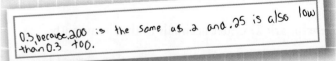

0.3, because .200 is the same as .2 and .25 is also low than 0.3 too.

Zachary's Work

Lourdes and Zachary should be asked to explain their thinking using different words or models to check to make sure they understand ordering these decimals.

Not Meeting the Benchmarks

Students do not meet this benchmark if they incorrectly identify the greatest number and either do not offer an explanation or provide an explanation that shows that they do not understand the meaning of these numbers.

Walter's work shows that he believes that 0.25 is the greatest decimal, but he offers no explanation.

Walter's Work

Olivia states that 0.200 is the greatest decimal because it has the most numbers. It is likely that Olivia is viewing these numbers as if they are whole numbers (e.g., 200 > 25 > 3).

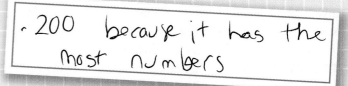

Olivia's Work

These students can benefit from continuing activities that involve representing and ordering small sets of decimal fractions, as suggested in Problem 1 above.

Adding Decimals

The goal for students' work on addition of decimals in Investigation 2 is for them to extend their understanding of all of the ideas they have been working on in this unit: representing and visualizing decimal fractions, using decimal equivalents or fraction equivalents, recognizing the place value of the digits, and comparing decimal numbers to one another and to landmarks such as $\frac{1}{2}$ and 1. The benchmark for this work, Benchmark 3, emphasizes a focus on representation and meaning of the numbers: Add decimal fractions through reasoning about place value, equivalents, and representations. In later grades, students will develop efficient and fluent strategies and algorithms for computation with decimals, but in this unit, addition is a context for students to apply their growing understanding of decimals.

Students come to this unit with fluent strategies for addition with whole numbers. They can build on these strategies, but they also need to sort out how to apply their knowledge about whole-number addition while focusing on the meaning of the decimal fractions. In fact, many of the same strategies students use to add whole numbers can be applied to decimals, and the addition combinations they know are just as important here as for their work with whole numbers.

Most fifth graders have one or more efficient addition strategies and are able to easily add three- and four-digit numbers, so that they can apply this knowledge as long as they also focus on the place value of the digits in the decimal fractions. Consider this example: $0.875 + 0.25$. Most Grade 5 students know that $875 + 25 = 900$. They may look quickly at these numbers, see a familiar combination, ignore the place value of the various digits, and incorrectly calculate the sum to be 0.9.

The challenge of this work is to help students use what they know about addition of whole numbers *and* to help them maintain and strengthen their understanding of the values of numbers less than one. For example, many students add whole numbers by place. This strategy also works well for

decimal fractions. A student may solve the problem above by adding the numbers in each place and then adding those partial sums.

$$0.8 + 0.2 = 1$$

$$0.07 + 0.05 = 0.12$$

$$1 + 0.12 + 0.005 = 1.125$$

Using rectangular grids to represent addition of fractions, as in the game *Fill Two*, helps students maintain their focus on the place value of the digits and, therefore, the meaning of the numbers. For example, a student may represent this problem on two grids.

Sample Student Work

This student may reason: "There are 125 thousandths left on the first grid, that's equal to $\frac{1}{8}$. You have $\frac{1}{4}$ on the other grid, so it will take half of that to fill up the first grid. So you have one whole grid and $\frac{1}{8}$ left on the other one, that's $1\frac{1}{8}$. In decimals, it's 1.125."

This student is reasoning about the sum according to the representation of the decimal fractions and knowledge of fraction-decimal equivalents. This is the kind of reasoning that students should be developing in this unit. As students become more experienced with the grids, they can begin to visualize this representation mentally, rather than actually shading in each number, although some students in Grade 5 will continue using the grids.

Estimation is another important aspect of the work on addition. Just as they do for whole-number computation, students should be developing the habit of looking at an addition expression and thinking about what a reasonable sum is before they start manipulating the numbers. For this problem, a student may think, "I know that $0.25 = \frac{1}{4}$, and 0.875 is more than $\frac{3}{4}$, so the sum has to be one plus a little more."

Often students are taught "rules" or "tricks" to add decimals, including lining up the decimal point. Sometimes, students are also taught to fill in blank spaces with zeros so that the problem looks like this:

$$\begin{array}{r} 0.875 \\ + \ 0.250 \\ \hline \end{array}$$

Underlying these rules are important understandings about decimal numbers—that 8 and 2 can be added because they both represent tenths, and that the decimal point is a notational mark that separates the integer portion of a number from the decimal part of that number. When students have a firm understanding of these ideas, they may also incorporate such rules into their repertoire of strategies, but at this point in their work on decimal computation, what is important is that they make sense of adding these numbers for themselves. For example, a student may come up with this same addition strategy because the student understands that 0.25 is equivalent to 0.250 and is more easily able to visualize adding these two numbers by thinking of adding 875 thousandths to 250 thousandths. It is this reasoning about the numbers and their representations, meanings, and relationships that is the focus of the work on addition in this unit.

End-of-Unit Assessment

Problem 1

Benchmark addressed:

Benchmark 2: Order decimals to the thousandths.

In order to meet the benchmark, students' work should show that they can:

• Place the numbers correctly relative to the landmarks in the chart;

• Place the numbers in the correct order.

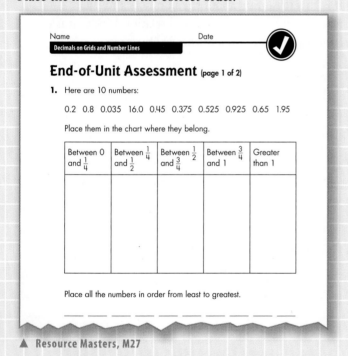

▲ **Resource Masters, M27**

Students are not asked to explain how they knew where to place the decimals because with so many numbers, there are too many decisions to explain. If they can sort them into the correct places in the chart and also put them in order, they demonstrate that they have met the benchmark.

Meeting the Benchmark

Students who meet the benchmark place all ten decimal numbers correctly on the chart, and either order all the numbers correctly or make only one or two errors in putting the numbers in order.

Hana places all the numbers correctly on the chart and makes one error in placing the numbers in order, reversing the order of 0.375 and 0.45. Hana knows that 0.375 and 0.45 fall between $\frac{1}{4}$ and $\frac{1}{2}$, and, given the rest of her response, it may be that the error is due to inattention rather than to lack of understanding.

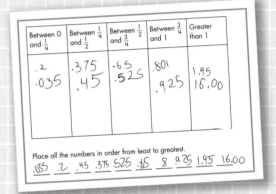

Hana's Work

Students have more difficulty with 0.035 than with any of the other numbers. Decimals with a 0 in the tenths place seem to be the last for students to completely understand as they sort out the meaning of zeros in decimal fractions. Students who place 0.035 correctly on the chart but then misplace it in the ordered list, usually as 0.2, 0.035, 0.375, 0.45, . . . with the rest of the list in the correct order, meet the benchmark. Students who do this show a strong understanding of the relative values of decimals and understands that 0.035 is less than $\frac{1}{4}$ but should practice shading in decimal fractions such as 0.035 and comparing it with 0.35.

Partially Meeting the Benchmark

Students who partially meet the benchmark make one or two errors in placing the decimal numbers on the chart and one or two errors in placing the numbers in order.

As previously described, the number most likely to cause confusion in this problem is 0.035. Students like Rachel have 0.035 in the incorrect spot on the chart and in sequence. These students often believe that the 0 in the tenths place can be ignored, so they incorrectly believe that the number should be placed between $\frac{1}{4}$ and $\frac{1}{2}$.

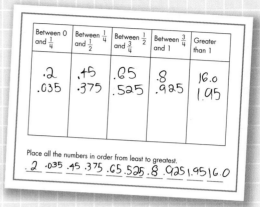

Charles's Work

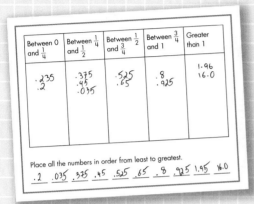

Rachel's Work

Rachel will benefit from shading in these numbers on a grid and comparing numbers such as 0.3, 0.03, and 0.30.

Not Meeting the Benchmark

Students who make numerous and significant errors in placing the numbers on the chart or in order do not meet the benchmark.

Charles has all the numbers placed correctly in the chart, but he has numerous errors when he places them in order. When putting the numbers in order, it appears that Charles may have just copied the numbers from the chart in the same order, although he does place 1.95 and 16.0 in the correct order relative to each other. Charles certainly shows some knowledge of the meaning of decimal fractions because he is able to place them all correctly with respect to the landmark fractions. Charles would benefit from representing these numbers on thousandths and hundredths grids and finding decimal equivalents. For example, if he recognizes that $0.45 = 0.450$ and can interpret 0.450 as 450 out of 1,000 equal parts, he may then be able to compare 0.45 and 0.375.

Problem 2
Benchmark addressed:

Benchmark 3: Add decimal fractions through reasoning about place value, equivalents, and representations.

In order to meet the benchmark, students' work should show that they can:

- Add the numbers correctly;

- Explain their solution in a way that shows that they understand the meaning of the numbers.

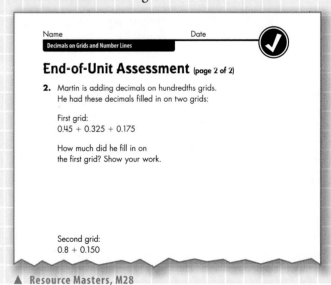

▲ Resource Masters, M28

Meeting the Benchmark

Students who meet the benchmark find the correct sums of each set of decimals and correctly combine the two sums.

$$0.45 + 0.325 + 0.175 = 0.95$$

$$0.8 + 0.150 = 0.95$$

$$0.95 + 0.95 = 1.9$$

They show clearly how they solved the problem.

Renaldo adds by place.

First grid:
.4 + .3 + .1 = .8
.05 + .02 + .07 = .14
.005 + .005 = .01
.8 + .14 + .01 = .95

Second grid:
.8 + .150 = .950
.9 + .9 = 1.8
1.8 + .05 + .05 = 1.9

Renaldo's Work

Renaldo's method clearly shows that he understands the value of the digits in each number. He adds mentally for the second grid and combines some steps in his final addition.

Note that some students solve parts of this problem mentally, and thus do not show any work for that part. For example, many students can easily add 0.8 and 0.150 by mentally adding the tenths. However, by inspecting the solution as a whole, it is generally apparent when students understand the values of the numbers by the way they break up the problem. Georgia breaks up some numbers by place but does much of the computation mentally.

.45 + .325 = .775
.775 + .175 = .950
.8 + .150 = .950

1.900
.900 + .900 = 1.800   1,900
.050 + .050 = 0.100

Georgia's Work

Yumiko carefully chooses which numbers to add first, choosing combinations that she knows and can calculate mentally. She carries out the final addition by using the carrying algorithm.

.325 + .175 = .500   1st grid   .150   2nd grid
.500 + .45 = .950   .950   + .8   .950
                                  .950
.950
+ .950
1.900

Yumiko's Work

Margaret thinks about the hundredths grid for her solution:

45 + 17 + 32 fills up 94 squares on the hundredths grid. 5 + 5 is one more square, so it's 95. The second grid is 95 too. I can just see that it's 9 tens and 5 hundredths. Then I took the 5 hundredths to fill up the first square. So it's 1.9 for both.

Margaret's Work

Although Margaret's wording is not always completely clear, her solution is correct, and she understands the values of the numbers and how to combine them. For example, when she writes "5 + 5 is one more square," she is combining 0.005 from 0.325 and 0.005 from 0.175 to get 0.01 (one more square on the hundredths grid).

Partially Meeting the Benchmark

Students who calculate an incorrect sum because of minor computation or place-value errors partially meet the benchmark. For many students, the most difficult part of the addition in this problem is adding 0.325 and 0.175. Some students break these numbers up correctly by place and add the tenths correctly but do not add the rest of the places correctly. For example, Alex determines that the sum of 0.025 and 0.075 is 0.01 instead of 0.1. The rest of his calculations are correct.

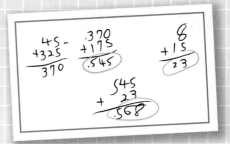

Mercedes's Work

Mercedes also does not notice that her final sum of 0.568 is not reasonable. She ends up with a total that is smaller than one of the addends (0.8).

Other students may attempt to break the numbers up by place, but lose track of the parts of the numbers or misrepresent their values, as Martin does.

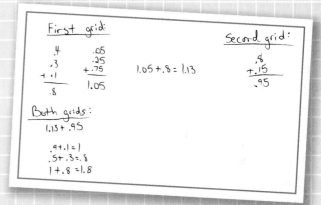

Martin's Work

Students like Alex may still be less confident about interpreting numbers in the thousandths, especially numbers with a zero in the tenths place. He can benefit from playing *Fill Two* and using grids to solve problems such as 0.075 + 0.025.

Not Meeting the Benchmark

Students who do not meet the benchmark do not get the correct sum, and their work shows misunderstandings about the values of decimals. Sometimes these students add the numbers as if they were whole numbers, and randomly place the decimal point in their partial sums or sums or simply place the decimal point at the beginning of every sum, as Mercedes does.

Alex's Work

Martin seems secure with tenths, but as soon as he operates with hundredths or thousandths, he frequently loses track of the places of the digits or carries out a familiar addition combination (such as 5 + 8 = 13) without regard for the places involved. He ends up with a final sum that is a reasonable estimate, in part because he ignores the one in 1.13 in his final computation.

These students may not be ready to add decimal fractions without more work on the meaning and representation of these numbers. They may need to work only with tenths and hundredths, representing them on grids and ordering small sets of Decimal Cards while referring to the grid representations.

Putting Decimals in Order

The class has just finished discussing how to label decimals on a number line in Session 1.3. In the next activity, students put decimals in order, using Set A of the Decimal Cards. The teacher circulates around the room as they work, observing different pairs of students. The teacher stops to watch Alex and Zachary.

First, Alex places the 0.1, 0.5, and 0.9 cards separated by spaces.

Alex: These are the closest to 0, $\frac{1}{2}$, and 1.

The boys place all the tenths cards in the correct order.

Zachary takes the 0.25 card and puts it after 0.9. The boys then quickly arrange the cards in this order:

0.1, 0.2, 0.3, 0.4, 0.5, 0.6, 0.7, 0.8, 0.9, 0.05, 0.15, 0.25, 0.35, 0.45, 0.55, 0.65, 0.75, 0.85, 0.95

Zachary: I'm not so sure about this. I know 0.5 is half. But I thought 0.25 was $\frac{1}{4}$, so it wouldn't be bigger.

The teacher has noticed a number of students making the same mistake, so she asks for the class's attention.

Teacher: As I'm watching you work, I notice that many of you are saying you're done. But I've also noticed that many of you think that because 0.5 just has one number after the decimal point, it's less than the decimals, like 0.25, that have two numbers after the decimal point. Think about what you've done with representing decimals on the grids, and also about everything you know about fractions and percents, and check your work. Thinking about money may help you, too.

The teacher turns back to Zachary and Alex.

Teacher: So what do you know about these numbers that could help you? Look at 0.45. Do you know what fraction or percent that is? How does that help you?

Alex: Oh yeah. It's 45%. So it's less than half.

Zachary: Look at this one. [He points to 0.85.] That's the same as 85%, so it's bigger than 0.8, because that's 80%.

The boys start reordering their cards correctly. The teacher moves on to Talisha and Hana. Hana has missed several weeks of school, and the teacher wants to check in with her. The girls are struggling with the task, and have placed only the 0.1, 0.2, and 0.5 cards. They are looking at 0.7.

Teacher: What do you know about the number on this card? What is it? What would it look like if you shaded it in on a grid? Is it more or less than $\frac{1}{2}$?

Hana: It's 7 tenths. It's more than 5 tenths.

Hana places the 0.7 card after 0.5, and the 0.9 card in the correct place, but she and Talisha seem puzzled by 0.95.

Teacher: Do you know what fraction this is equivalent to? Or what percent? Think about what it would look like on a grid.

Hana: It's $\frac{95}{100}$. That's 95%. It's almost 1!

Talisha: It would be 95 out of 100 on the hundredths grid and 0.9 would be 90 out of a hundred.

Hana correctly places the 0.95 card. The teacher works with Hana and Talisha a few more minutes. Then the teacher goes back to check with Alex and Zachary. They have placed all the cards except for 0.05.

Zachary: I think this is the same as 0.5. The zeroes don't matter. Like 0.5 and 0.50 are the same thing.

Alexander: I'm not so sure about that, but I don't know what's right.

Teacher: Let's look at some of your other cards, like this one, 0.35. How would you say this number? What does the 3 mean? What does the 5 mean?

Zachary: 35 hundredths.

Alex: 3 is 3 tenths and 5 is 5 hundredths.

Teacher: What about 0.25? What do the digits mean?

Alex: 25 hundredths. And it's the same as 2 tenths and 5 hundredths. If you color it in on the tenths grid, it's 2 and $\frac{1}{2}$ tenths.

Zachary: Now, I think the 5 in 0.05 is in the hundredths place. So it's five hundredths.

Alex: Oh yeah. It's sorta like money. 0.25 would be a quarter and 0.05 would be a nickel. And I guess 0.1 would be a dime. So 0.05 is smallest.

As the teacher works with pairs of students and the whole class, she finds that many of her students need to review what they know about the meaning of decimals. The teacher prompts them to use what they know about fraction-percent-decimal equivalents, about representing decimals on hundredths grids, about the relationship of the numbers to 0, $\frac{1}{2}$, and 1, and about the place value of the digits. Although some students find money helpful as a model, many students think of 25¢ as 25 pennies (or two dimes and five pennies), not as parts of one dollar. Therefore, the teacher hesitates to use money as a model unless students bring it up themselves. Alex and Zachary's questions about the meaning of the 0 in 0.05 are not unusual. Just as in earlier grades, students sometimes did not know how to interpret zeros in whole numbers, students now must revisit this issue with decimals, recognizing which digits represent tenths, hundredths, thousandths, and so on even when there is a 0 in one or more places.

Dialogue Box

Filling in the Fraction-to-Decimal Division Table

In Session 1.8, the teacher has introduced the activity and students have filled in all the equivalents for 0.5 in the table. As the students begin to work on their own, the teacher wants to emphasize that students already know many of the decimal equivalents from their work with fractions and percents.

Teacher: As you begin working on your own, remember that the top row is the numerator and the left side is the denominator. You already know many of these equivalents. Think about what the fraction is, what the percent equivalent is, and what that would be as a decimal. Also think about fraction equivalents, such as $\frac{1}{3}$ and $\frac{2}{6}$. All these things will help you fill in the chart. Remember, for today just work on rows 1–6, 8, 10, and 12.

As students begin working, the teacher circulates and listens as students fill in the chart.

Tamira: The 2 row has a pattern! It's half, whole, half, whole, half, whole, like that. So it's one half, one, one and a half, two, two and a half, three.

Felix: The 10 row is easy, too. $\frac{1}{10}$ is 10%, so the decimal is 0.1. Then it just goes up by one tenth each time, one tenth, two tenths, three tenths, like that until you get to 1. Then it just starts over—one and one tenth, one and two tenths, one and three tenths.

Avery: When you fill in the 5 row it's like counting by 2's, only it's really 0.2. So it's point two, point four, point six, point eight, point ten. Oh wait. Not 0.10—one!

Hana: I started with thirds, but I wasn't sure. So I did the easy part—$\frac{3}{3}$ is 1, $\frac{6}{3}$ is 2, $\frac{9}{3}$ is 3, $\frac{12}{3}$ is 4. But I couldn't figure out what $\frac{1}{3}$ was so I used the calculator. It shows 0.33333333. That's kind of like $33\frac{1}{3}$%, but not exactly. And that means $\frac{2}{3}$ is 0.66666666.

Shandra: I did the 4 row, and it was easy too. $\frac{1}{4}$ is 25% and so the decimal is 0.25, then we already did 0.5, and $\frac{3}{4}$ is 0.75.

Renaldo: I'm still not sure about sixths, but I know $\frac{2}{6}$ is $\frac{1}{3}$, so that's 0.33333333, and $\frac{4}{6}$ is $\frac{2}{3}$ so that's 0.66666666.

Alex: I'm trying to figure out the 8 row, and I just don't know what to do.

Teacher: Does knowing the percent equivalent help you?

[Alex shakes his head no.]

Teacher: OK, so let's use the calculator. Do you remember what to do?

Alex: Yeah. I do 1 divided by 8. It says 0.125.

He writes 0.125 in the table and calculates $\frac{2}{8}$ on the calculator. He writes 0.25 in the table and mutters, "Oh yeah, it's the same as $\frac{1}{4}$." Then he calculates $\frac{3}{8}$ on the calculator and writes in 0.375. He sees that 0.5 is already filled in.

Teacher: Alex, do you think you have enough information now to fill in the rest of the row without using the calculator?

Alex: I . . . I think so. I think 5 divided by 8 is going to be 0.625, but I just want to check on the calculator and make sure.

The teacher notices that many students are taking time to think about the fraction and percent equivalents, and using patterns they find to fill in the rows of the chart. After students fill in the decimals with which they are most familiar, the teacher will encourage students to continue thinking about how fraction equivalents such as $\frac{2}{8} = \frac{1}{4}$ help them fill in the chart.

Patterns on the Division Table

Students have spent most of the day's math lesson in Session 1.8 filling in decimals on *Student Activity Book* page 35. As they finish, the teacher asks them to look at the chart, look for patterns, and think about why those patterns occur. At first, students offer what they notice about individual rows on the chart, such as the 2, 4, 6, 8, 0 pattern in the tenths row. After discussing a few of these, the teacher focuses students' attention on the table as a whole, encouraging them not only to identify patterns but also to think about why these patterns occur.

Teacher: You've done some good thinking while you filled in these charts. Many of you found patterns as you filled in each row or column, but now we're going to think about the chart as a whole. What patterns did you notice on the whole chart?

Mitch: The 1 is on a diagonal across the page.

Teacher: Anyone have any thoughts about why that happens?

Georgia: Well, it's because if you start up in the corner, the fraction is $\frac{1}{1}$. If you go one over and one down it's $\frac{2}{2}$, then $\frac{3}{3}$. The numerator and the denominator are the same, so that equals 1. It's always true.

Yumiko: When you go across the rows, the decimals get bigger.

Teacher: Why is that true? Why do the numbers get bigger?

Olivia: The numbers going across are the numerators, and they get bigger. So the decimal is going to get bigger, because the denominator stays the same, and there are more of the pieces. It's like when we did the percent equivalents, $\frac{1}{5}$ is 20%, $\frac{2}{5}$ is 40%, like that.

Teacher: Nice. Olivia remembers what we did when we worked with fractions.

Avery: I just realized when you go down a column, it's the same thing, only the numbers get smaller. [To the teacher] I know, I know, you want to know why. It's the same thing as Olivia said, only the opposite. The numerator stays the same, but the denominator gets bigger, so there's the same number of pieces, but the pieces are smaller, like $\frac{2}{3}$, then $\frac{2}{4}$, then $\frac{2}{5}$. It's always two of the pieces, but thirds are bigger than fourths and fourths are bigger than fifths and it keeps going.

By asking students to look at the chart as a whole, the teacher helps students focus on mathematical relationships she knows they have the background and experience to consider and explain. Some of the patterns within rows are also accessible to fifth graders (e.g., the halves, fourths, and tenths rows), but the mathematical relationships that result in some of the other patterns (e.g., the sevenths, ninths, and elevenths rows), although interesting to fifth graders, are not as accessible to them. This teacher spends more time on mathematical relationships that students can explain by using their knowledge of fraction-percent-decimal equivalents.

Adding Decimals: The Jeweler's Gold

In Session 2.2, students have been working in groups to solve the problem 1.14 + 0.3 + 0.085. They created posters explaining their solution. As the teacher circulated among the small groups, listening to assess what students understand about the value of decimals and how to add them, the teacher noticed three different answers: 2.02 grams, 2.29 grams, and 1.525 grams. To start the class discussion, the teacher asks four groups to post their work at the front of the room—two of these have incorrect sums and two are different approaches that resulted in the correct sum.

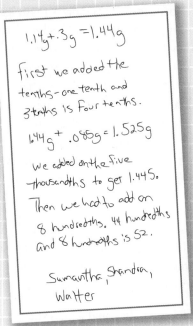

Sample Student Work

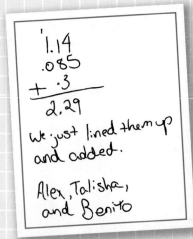

Sample Student Work

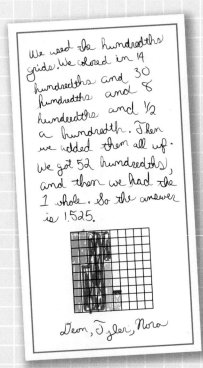

Sample Student Work

Sample Student Work

Teacher: Let's look at these four solutions. I think everyone got one of these answers. How many people got 2.02 grams? [About $\frac{1}{3}$ of the students raise their hands.] 2.29 grams? [Less than $\frac{1}{4}$ of the students raise their hands.] 1.525 grams? [About $\frac{1}{2}$ the students raise their hands.] Can they all be right?

A few students appear to be seriously considering this, because the computation on each poster appears to be correct. But after a brief discussion, students agree that just because they are using decimals, there still cannot be more than one correct answer.

Teacher: So let's figure out which answer is correct. Who has questions about any of these solutions?

Hana: It looks like Talisha's group did something different with the 3 tenths and the 85 thousandths when they lined them up. They have the 1, 8 and 3 lined up. It seems like they're adding different things.

Benito: Since zero plus something is the same thing, we just ignored the 0 in .085.

Hana: But that doesn't make sense! The 0 is showing there are 0 tenths in the number and you can't add tenths and hundredths like that. [She pauses.] Can you?

Tyler: It sort of looks like Stuart's group did the same thing though. They added everything up, but their answer is too big. The numbers have a one and then a bunch of little parts. It couldn't be more than two.

Stuart: Our answer's too big? It's not as big as Samantha's group!

[Students start talking to one another, trying to figure out what Stuart means.]

Teacher: Hold on. All these comments are important and they are about different things. Let's look at Stuart's comment first. Which number is greater, 2.02 or 1.525?

Stuart: Oh! I got confused a second. Our answer is bigger because 2 is bigger than 1. It's just all those numbers, I thought it was a bigger number.

Teacher: Yes, it gets confusing sometimes. So let's go back to Hana's question. Did Olivia's and Alex's groups mix up things when they added? What do people think?

Samantha: Me and Shandra and Walter talked about that, too. First we just added them up and got 2.02. Then Shandra said that answer didn't make sense. It was too big.

Shandra: That's right! I asked them about 0.085 and said it didn't seem like it was very big. It's just like zero almost.

Deon: Look, when we shaded it in on the hundredths grid, you can see how small it is. It's not even one tenth.

Teacher: Good point, Shandra, and Deon, that really helps us, I think, to look at your group's picture. Let's think about that for a minute, instead of trying to figure out the answer. What numbers are these decimals close to? 0? $\frac{1}{2}$? 1?

The class decides 1.14 is close to 1, 0.3 is close to $\frac{1}{2}$, and 0.089 is close to 0, so the sum would be around $1\frac{1}{2}$.

Teacher: So our answer should be around 1.5. How can we figure out what the sum is?

Walter: Well, once we figured out our first answer was wrong, then we added 1.14 and 0.3. That's 1.44. You can't just add the 3 to the 4 because it's 3 tenths and 4 hundredths. You have to add the 3 to the 1 in the 14 hundredths. We thought about 0.3 as being the same as 30 hundredths.

[A number of students nod their heads as if this explanation (0.3 = 0.30) makes sense to them.]

Walter: Then we just did the same thing with 85 thousandths. Instead of adding 44 and 85, we thought of 0.44 being the same as 0.440 and added that way. Although that's not what we show on the chart. But, you have to add the same thing to the same thing. You can't just line them up and add however you want.

Teacher: It seems like many people were making sense of what Walter was saying his group did with equivalent decimals—that 3 tenths is the same as 30 hundredths and 44 hundredths is the same as 440 thousandths. Even though they didn't use 0.300 and 0.440 on their chart, they still lined it up so that they were adding tenths to tenths and hundredths to hundredths.

Stuart: I think I kinda get it. It's like when you add 295 + 47. You add the 5 and 7 because they're both in the ones place, and add 9 tens and 4 tens, because they're both in the tens place. You wouldn't add 2 and 4, because 2 is hundreds and 4 is tens.

Nora: If you just think of all of them as hundredths, it's easy to add. That's what we did on the hundredths grid. You know you just have the 1, so then it's 14 hundredths and 30 hundredths and 8 hundredths. And we knew that 5 thousandths is $\frac{1}{2}$ a hundredth. So then you just add them.

Teacher: You're going to keep practicing adding decimals, so it's something to keep thinking about. When you add decimals, you have to think about the value of each digit—whether it's tenths, hundredths, or thousandths. Like Stuart said, it's just like thinking about the place value of the digits in whole numbers—a 2 in the ones place doesn't mean the same thing as a 2 in the hundreds place, and a 2 in the tenths place doesn't mean the same thing as a 2 in the thousandths place.

The teacher knows that when students first work on adding decimal fractions, they sometimes try to apply strategies they know for adding whole numbers, but follow the form of these strategies without keeping track of the values of the digits. By emphasizing the meaning of each number, estimating a reasonable sum, and referring to representations of the numbers on the grids, this teacher helps students stay focused on the place value of each digit.

Dialogue Box

Student Strategies for Adding Decimals

During Session 2.3, the teacher notices that a number of students are mixing up place values to add decimals. For the discussion at the end of the session, the teacher has identified four students who are keeping the place value of each digit clear as they add the numbers. She charts their strategies for adding 0.625, 0.75, and 0.08 before the discussion begins and asks them to explain them. These solutions are on chart paper:

$$\begin{array}{r} 0.625 \\ +\ 0.75 \\ \hline 1.375 \\ +\ 0.8 \\ \hline 2.175 \end{array} \qquad \begin{array}{r} 0.8 \\ 0.75 \\ +\ 0.625 \\ \hline 2.175 \end{array}$$

0.8 + 0.75 + 0.625

2.1 + 0.07 + 0.005 = 2.175

0.625 + 0.8 = 1.425
(1.425 + 0.75)
1.425 + 0.7 = 2.125
2.125 + 0.05 = 2.175

Teacher: I've asked several students to explain how they added these three numbers. You can see their solutions on the chart. Each one is going to explain how they solved the problem. As you listen to them, try to understand how they solved the problem, and think about whether you solved it the same way or a different way. Nora?

Nora: I added the decimals one at a time. I started with 0.625, because it was the longest one, and added 0.75. It was easy to add those numbers, then I added the 0.8. It was easy to add those numbers too.

Teacher: Nora, how did you know where to put the 0.75, and the 0.8? It seems like you were thinking about that.

Nora: Yeah, it's like we talked about yesterday. You have to add the tenths to the tenths, and the hundredths to the hundredths. So I put the 75 hundredths right under the 62 hundredths. I knew the 5 thousandths would stay the same, then I added the others. The same for 8 tenths, I put it under the 3 tenths. That was easy to add—I actually thought what's 13 + 8 and it's 21, but of course it's 21 tenths, that's 2.1.

Teacher: Deon?

Deon: I just lined all of three of them up, and added. I did the same thing Nora did—I just made sure the tenths were lined up—once they were lined up, the other ones were lined up too. Then I just added.

Olivia: [explaining the third example]: I guess I did the same thing, but it doesn't look like it. First I added all my tenths, then the hundredths, then the thousandths.

Renaldo: I tried the same thing, but I got confused, because I put down 5 and 2 as 0.7, and then put down 0.5. I got 3.3, but I knew that sum was too big, but I couldn't figure out what I did wrong.

Teacher: So let's ask Olivia how she kept track of that.

Olivia: I just had to keep asking myself, "What is this 5 and 2? Are they tenths? No. Are they hundredths? Yes. So that makes it 0.07. Same thing for the five in 0.625. I knew it was thousandths, so I wrote 0.005.

Teacher: Good thinking. When you are adding decimals, we need to think about what both Renaldo and Olivia said. Renaldo knew that 3.3 was too big, and it's really important to have an idea about what the sum should be. Olivia also paid careful attention to what she was adding, making sure that she added tenths to tenths, hundredths to hundredths, and thousandths to thousandths, and then she put them all together. We have time for one more strategy. Rachel?

Rachel: This is the way I always add with regular numbers. I start with one number, then I break up the other one and add it on in parts. So I did $0.625 + 0.8 = 1.425$—that was an easy one I could do in my head. But I couldn't add the 0.75 in my head, so I made it 0.7 and 0.05. $1.425 + 0.7$ is 2.125, then I added 0.05, so it's 2.175.

Martin: Wait! When you did $2.125 + 0.05$, why isn't it 2.130? Doesn't $25 + 5 = 30$?

Rachel: Nope. I did the same thing everyone else has been talking about—I made sure I added the same thing to the same thing. In 2.125, the 2 is in the hundredths place, so that's what I had to add the 0.05 to, so it's 2.175.

It is not unusual for students just learning to add decimals to see what appears to be an easy combination and add those numbers, forgetting about the place value of the digits. This is what Martin brings up when he describes adding 25 and 5. The teacher selected several students to explain their addition strategies because she knew that they had a strong understanding of the place value of decimals, and she wanted the whole class to hear their explanations while giving other students, like Martin, an opportunity to talk through some of their questions and confusions.

Student Math Handbook

The *Student Math Handbook* pages related to this unit are pictured on the following pages. This book is designed to be used flexibly: as a resource for students doing classwork, as a book students can take home for reference while doing homework and playing math games with their families, and as a reference for families to better understand the work their children are doing in class.

When students take the *Student Math Handbook* home, they and their families can discuss these pages together to reinforce or enhance students' understanding of the mathematical concepts and games in this unit.

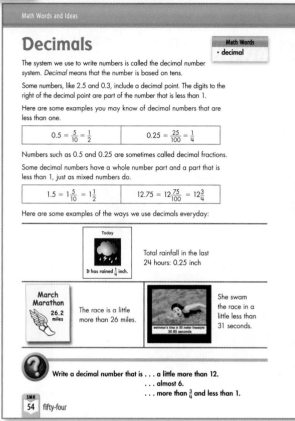

Decimals

Math Words
· decimal

The system we use to write numbers is called the decimal number system. *Decimal* means that the number is based on tens.

Some numbers, like 2.5 and 0.3, include a decimal point. The digits to the right of the decimal point are part of the number that is less than 1.

Here are some examples you may know of decimal numbers that are less than one.

$$0.5 = \frac{5}{10} = \frac{1}{2} \qquad 0.25 = \frac{25}{100} = \frac{1}{4}$$

Numbers such as 0.5 and 0.25 are sometimes called decimal fractions.

Some decimal numbers have a whole number part and a part that is less than 1, just as mixed numbers do.

$$1.5 = 1\frac{5}{10} = 1\frac{1}{2} \qquad 12.75 = 12\frac{75}{100} = 12\frac{3}{4}$$

Here are some examples of the ways we use decimals everyday:

Today
It has rained $\frac{1}{4}$ inch.

Total rainfall in the last 24 hours: 0.25 inch

March Marathon 26.2 miles
The race is a little more than 26 miles.

swimmer's time in 50 meter freestyle 30.85 seconds
She swam the race in a little less than 31 seconds.

? Write a decimal number that is . . . a little more than 12.
. . . almost 6.
. . . more than $\frac{3}{4}$ and less than 1.

SMH 54 fifty-four

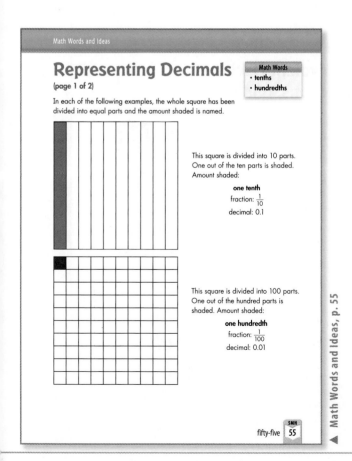

Representing Decimals
(page 1 of 2)

Math Words
· tenths
· hundredths

In each of the following examples, the whole square has been divided into equal parts and the amount shaded is named.

This square is divided into 10 parts. One out of the ten parts is shaded. Amount shaded:

one tenth
fraction: $\frac{1}{10}$
decimal: 0.1

This square is divided into 100 parts. One out of the hundred parts is shaded. Amount shaded:

one hundredth
fraction: $\frac{1}{100}$
decimal: 0.01

fifty-five **SMH** 55

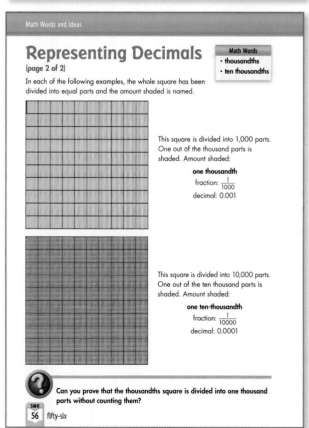

Representing Decimals
(page 2 of 2)

Math Words
· thousandths
· ten thousandths

In each of the following examples, the whole square has been divided into equal parts and the amount shaded is named.

This square is divided into 1,000 parts. One out of the thousand parts is shaded. Amount shaded:

one thousandth
fraction: $\frac{1}{1000}$
decimal: 0.001

This square is divided into 10,000 parts. One out of the ten thousand parts is shaded. Amount shaded:

one ten-thousandth
fraction: $\frac{1}{10000}$
decimal: 0.0001

? Can you prove that the thousandths square is divided into one thousand parts without counting them?

SMH 56 fifty-six

Math Words and Ideas

Place Value of Decimals

Math Words
· **decimal point**

As with whole numbers, the value of a digit changes depending on its place in a decimal number.

thousands place	hundreds place	tens place	ones place	·	tenths place	hundredths place	thousandths place

decimal point

In these three examples the digit 5 has different **values:**

0.5   0.45   0.625

The digit 5 in the **tenths place** represents $\frac{5}{10}$.

The digit 5 in the **hundredths place** represents $\frac{5}{100}$.

The digit 5 in the **thousandths place** represents $\frac{5}{1,000}$.

Look at the values of the digits in this number:

1.375 (one and three hundred seventy-five thousandths or $1\frac{375}{1,000}$)

1   the digit 1 represents one whole
0.3   the digit 3 represents three tenths
0.07   the digit 7 represents seven hundredths
0.005   the digit 5 represents five thousandths

$$1.375 = 1 + 0.3 + 0.07 + 0.005$$

fifty-seven **SMH 57**

Math Words and Ideas

Reading and Writing Decimals

The number of digits after the decimal point tells how to read a decimal number.

0 . __
one digit

0.4	0.5	0.7
four tenths	five tenths	seven tenths

0 . __ __
two digits

0.40	0.05	0.35
forty hundredths	five hundredths	thirty-five hundredths

0 . __ __ __
three digits

0.400	0.005	0.250
four hundred thousandths	five thousandths	two hundred fifty thousandths

For decimals greater than one, read the whole number, say "and" for the decimal point, and then read the decimal.

3 . 75
three and seventy-five hundredths

10 . 5
ten and five tenths

200 . 05
two hundred and five hundredths

17 . 345
seventeen and three hundred forty-five thousandths

 Say this number: 40.35
Write this number: three hundred five and four tenths

SMH 58 fifty-eight

Math Words and Ideas

Equivalent Decimals, Fractions, and Percents

(page 1 of 2)

You can describe the shaded part of this 10 × 10 square in different ways.

How many tenths are shaded?
0.5   (5 out of 10 columns are shaded)

How many hundredths are shaded?
0.50   (50 out of 100 squares are shaded)

These decimals are equal: 0.5 = 0.50

There are many ways to represent the same part of a whole with decimals, fractions, and percents.

$$0.5 = 0.50 = \frac{1}{2} = \frac{5}{10} = \frac{50}{100} = 50\%$$

Now look at this 10 × 10 square.

How many tenths are shaded?
0.2   (2 out of 10 columns are shaded)

How many hundredths are shaded?
0.20   (20 out of 100 squares are shaded)

$$0.2 = 0.20 = \frac{2}{10} = \frac{1}{5} = \frac{20}{100} = 20\%$$

 How many tenths are shaded?
How many hundredths are shaded?
What fractional parts are shaded?
What percent is shaded?

fifty-nine **SMH 59**

Math Words and Ideas

Equivalent Decimals, Fractions, and Percents

(page 2 of 2)

Find the decimal equivalents for $\frac{1}{8}$, $\frac{4}{8}$, and $\frac{5}{8}$.

Several students used different strategies to find the solution to this problem.

Tavon's solution
I used my calculator to figure out $\frac{1}{8}$. The fraction $\frac{1}{8}$ is the same as 1 ÷ 8, and the answer is 0.125.

$$\frac{1}{8} = 0.125$$

Margaret's solution
I got the same answer a different way.
$\frac{1}{8}$ is half of $\frac{1}{4}$ and $\frac{1}{4}$ = 25%. So, $\frac{1}{8}$ is half of 25%. That's $12\frac{1}{2}\%$, or 0.125.

$$\frac{1}{8} = 0.125$$

Avery's solution
To solve $\frac{4}{8}$, I just thought about equivalent fractions. $\frac{4}{8}$ is really easy because it is the same as $\frac{1}{2}$.

$$\frac{4}{8} = \frac{1}{2} = 0.5$$

Samantha's solution
I imagined $\frac{5}{8}$ shaded on a 10 × 10 square. That fills up $\frac{1}{2}$ plus one more eighth.

$$\frac{5}{8} = \frac{1}{2} + \frac{1}{8}$$
$$= 50\% + 12\frac{1}{2}\%$$
$$= 62\frac{1}{2}\%$$
$$\frac{5}{8} = 0.625$$

 Find the decimal equivalents for these fractions:
$$\frac{6}{8} \qquad \frac{7}{8} \qquad \frac{8}{8}$$

SMH 60 sixty

---

148 **UNIT 6** | **Decimals on Grids and Number Lines**

Comparing and Ordering Decimals (page 1 of 2)

Which is larger, 0.35 or 0.6?

Rachel's solution

Rachel used 10 × 10 squares to compare the decimals.

I thought 0.35 was bigger because it has more numbers in it. But when I drew the picture, I saw that 0.6 is the same as $\frac{60}{100}$, which is more than $\frac{35}{100}$.

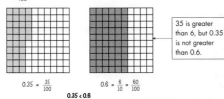

> 35 is greater than 6, but 0.35 is not greater than 0.6.

$$0.35 = \frac{35}{100} \qquad 0.6 = \frac{6}{10} = \frac{60}{100}$$

0.35 < 0.6

Three students ran a 400-meter race.

Place their times in order from fastest to slowest.

Walter looked at place value to put the times in order.

NAME	TIME (SECONDS)
CHARLES	51.12
MARTIN	50.90
STUART	51.04

Walter's solution

First Place: Martin, 50.90 seconds

Second Place: Stuart, 51.04 seconds

Third Place: Charles, 51.12 seconds

I looked at the whole number parts. Since 50 < 51, 50.90 is the fastest time.

> The least number of seconds is the fastest time.

Stuart and Charles each finished in a little more than 51 seconds. 4 hundredths is less than 12 hundredths, so Stuart was faster than Charles.

Comparing and Ordering Decimals (page 2 of 2)

What is the order of these decimals from least to greatest?

0.8	0.55	0.625
eight tenths	fifty-five hundredths	six hundred twenty-five thousandths

Samantha used a number line to put the decimals in order.

Samantha's solution

I used a number line from 0 to 1.

I marked the tenths on the number line and I knew where to put 0.8.

0.55 is between 0.50 and 0.60, so I put it between 0.5 and 0.6.

0.625 is a little more than 0.6.

0.55 < 0.625 < 0.8

Which is larger, 0.65 or 0.4?
Which is larger, 0.4 or 0.375?

Adding Decimals (page 1 of 3)

Deon, Alicia, and Zachary used different strategies to add these decimals.

$$0.4 + 0.25 =$$

Deon's solution

I used different colors to shade the decimals on a 10 × 10 square.

*The total is 6 tenths and 5 hundredths, or **0.65**.*

Alicia's solution

$$\begin{array}{r} 0.40 \\ + 0.25 \\ \hline \mathbf{0.65} \end{array}$$

0.4 is the same as 0.40.

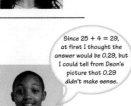

> *0.4 is close to $\frac{1}{2}$ and 0.25 is the same as $\frac{1}{4}$, so I knew the answer should be close to $\frac{3}{4}$, or 0.75.*

Zachary's solution

So, I added by place. I added the tenths, and then the hundredths.

0.4 is 4 tenths and 0 hundredths.

0.25 is 2 tenths and 5 hundredths.

0.4 + 0.2 = 0.6

*6 tenths and 5 hundredths is **0.65**.*

> *Since 25 + 4 = 29, at first I thought the answer would be 0.29, but I could tell from Deon's picture that 0.29 didn't make sense.*

Adding Decimals (page 2 of 3)

Shandra, Joshua, Nora, and Lourdes solved this addition problem in different ways.

What is the sum of these decimals?

0.6	0.125	0.45
six tenths	one hundred twenty-five thousandths	forty-five hundredths

Shandra's solution

I broke up the numbers and added by place.

First I added all of the tenths. Next I added the hundredths. Then I added everything together.

$$0.6 + 0.1 + 0.4 = 1.1$$
$$0.02 + 0.05 = 0.07$$
$$1.1 + 0.07 + 0.005 = \mathbf{1.175}$$

> I knew that the answer would be more than 1 because in the tenths I saw 0.6 and 0.4, which add up to 1.

Joshua's solution

I used equivalents. I just thought of all the numbers as thousandths; then I added them.

$$0.6 = 0.600$$
$$0.45 = 0.450$$
$$600 + 450 = 1,050$$
$$1,050 + 125 = 1,175$$

*Since 1,000 thousandths is 1, the answer is **1.175**.*

Math Words and Ideas

Adding Decimals (page 3 of 3)

$$0.6 + 0.125 + 0.45 = \underline{\ ?\ }$$

Walter's solution

I did it kind of like Joshua, but I lined up the numbers and then added.

```
  0.600
  0.125
+ 0.450
  1.100
  0.070
+ 0.005
  1.175
```

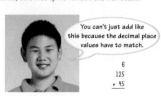

You can't just add like this because the decimal place values have to match.

```
    6
  125
+  45
```

Lourdes' solution

I split up 0.45 into 4 tenths and 5 hundredths.

$$0.45 = 0.4 + 0.05$$

```
  0.4      0.050
+ 0.6    + 0.125
  1.0      0.175

      1.175
```

You may notice that you are using the same strategies to add decimals that you used to add whole numbers. You can review those addition strategies on pages 8–9 in this handbook.

 0.65 + 0.3 = _____   0.375 + 0.2 = _____

sixty-five **65**

Games

Close to 1

You need

• Decimal Cards, Sets A and B
• *Close to 1* Recording Sheet

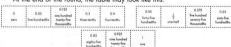

Play with 1 or 2 other players.

The object of the game is to choose cards whose sum is as close to 1 as possible.

1. Deal five cards in the middle. Each player uses any or all of these cards to make a total that is as close to 1 as possible. (Everyone uses the same five cards.)

2. Write the numbers and the sum on the *Close to 1* Recording Sheet.

3. Find your score. The score for the round is the difference between the sum and 1. (Your sum can be under or over 1.)

4. When all players have come up with a sum and a score, compare your results with each other.

5. Put all five cards in the discard pile.

6. Deal five new cards.

7. After five rounds, total your scores. The player with the lowest score wins.

Variations

Follow the rules above, making one or more of these adjustments:

• Make four wild cards to use for play.
• Each player gets his or her own five cards.

G1

Games

Decimal Double Compare

You need

• Decimal Cards, Set A (2 sets)

Play with a partner.

1. Mix the cards and deal them evenly so that each player has the same number of cards. Place the cards facedown in front of you.

2. Each player turns over the top two cards in his or her stack.

3. Look at your two numbers and your partner's two numbers. Decide which player has the larger sum.

4. Whoever has the larger sum takes all of the cards that have been turned over and places them at the bottom of his or her stack.

5. If both sums are the same, each player keeps his or her cards. Turn over the next two cards.

6. Play for a given amount of time or until one player has all of the cards. The player with more cards wins.

Variations

Follow the rules above, making one or more of these adjustments:

• The person with the smaller sum takes the cards.
• Include Set B of the Decimal Cards.
• Add new cards. Use either "wild cards" (which could be any number) or "equivalent cards," such as 0.50 or 0.950.

G4

Games

Decimals In Between

You need

• Decimal Cards, Sets A and B

Play with a partner.

1. Find the three game cards labeled 0, $\frac{1}{2}$, and 1. Place these cards on the table (see picture below).

2. Mix the Decimal Cards. Deal six to each player.

3. Players take turns placing a card so that it touches another card in one of these ways:
   • to the right of 0   • to the left of 1
   • on either side of $\frac{1}{2}$ • on top of any equivalent

   As you play a card, read the decimal aloud.

4. Cards must be placed in increasing order, from left to right. A card may not be placed between two cards that are touching.

| 0 zero | 0.05 five-hundredths | | 0.45 forty-five hundredths | $\frac{1}{2}$ one-half | | 1 one |

   In the example above, the 0.025 card may not be placed between the 0 and 0.05 cards. It cannot be played in this round.

5. Your goal is to place as many cards as you can. The round is over when neither player can place any more cards. Your score is the number of cards left in your hand.

   At the end of the round, the table may look like this:

| 0 zero | 0.05 five-hundredths | 0.125 one hundred twenty-five thousandths | 0.3 three-tenths | 0.4 four-tenths | 0.45 forty-five hundredths | $\frac{1}{2}$ one-half | 0.575 five hundred seventy-five thousandths | 0.65 sixty-five hundredths |

| 0.85 eighty-five hundredths | 0.925 nine hundred twenty-five thousandths | 1 one |

   In this sample round, Player 1 could not play 0.25 or 0.6. Player 1 has a score of 2. Player 2 could not play 0.025. Player 2 has a score of 1.

6. At the end of five rounds, the player with the lower score wins.

G5

Fill Two

You need

- Decimal Cards, Set A (1 set)
- Hundredths Grids for *Fill Two* (1 sheet per player)
- crayons or markers (2 or more colors for each player)

Play with a partner.

1 Mix the cards and turn the deck facedown. Turn over the top four cards and place them faceup in a row.

2 The goal is to shade in two of your grids as completely as possible.

3 Players take turns. On your turn, choose one of the faceup cards, color in that amount on either grid, and write the number below the grid. You may not color in an amount that would more than fill a grid, and you may not split an amount to color in parts of two grids.

4 After one of the four cards has been picked, replace it with the top card from the deck.

5 Change colors for each turn so that you can see the different decimals. As you write the number below each square, use plus (+) signs between the numbers, making an equation that will show the total colored in on each grid.

6 If all of the cards showing are greater than the spaces left on your grids, you lose your turn until a usable card is turned up.

7 The game is over when neither player can choose a card. Players add all of the numbers they have colored in on each grid and then combine those sums to get a final total for both grids. The winner is the player whose final sum is closer to 2.

Variation: *Fill Four*

Follow the rules for *Fill Two* except for the following changes:

- Use Decimal Cards Set A and Set B (1 set of each).
- Each player fills four grids during a game. On a turn, you may color in the amount on any grid that has enough room.
- The winner is the player whose final sum is closer to 4.

Hundredths Grids for Fill Two

Smaller to Larger

You need

- Decimal Cards, Sets A and B (1 set of each for 2 players, 2 sets of each for 3 or 4 players)

Play with a partner or in a small group.

1 Mix together all of the Decimal Cards.

2 Each player draws a 3 × 3 grid for a game mat, with spaces large enough for Decimal Cards to fit inside.

3 Mix the combined deck and place it facedown between the players.

4 Players take turns. On your turn, draw the top card from the pile and decide where to place it on your game mat. The numbers must be in increasing order, from left to right in each row and from top to bottom in each column.

5 If you draw a card that you cannot place because of the numbers already on your game mat, you must keep the card in a pile and lose your turn.

Example:

Suppose that after six turns, your game mat looks like this. You draw 0.15 and it cannot be played because 0.375 is already in the lowest place on the board. Put the 0.15 card in your pile of cards that cannot be played.

6 If you are unsure which of two numbers is larger, discuss them with other players.

7 The game is over when each player has filled all nine spaces.

8 The winner is the player who has fewer cards that cannot be played. If no player fills all nine spaces of the gameboard, the player with more cards placed on the gameboard is the winner.

Index